Usborne
Illustrated
Elementary
MATH
Dictionary

Usborne Quicklinks

The Usborne Quicklinks Website is packed with thousands of links to all the best websites on the internet. The websites include information, video clips, sounds, games and animations that support and enhance the information in Usborne internet-linked books.

To visit the recommended websites for the Illustrated Elementary Math Dictionary, go to the Usborne Quicklinks Website at www.usborne-quicklinks.com and enter the keywords: elementary math

Internet safety

When using the internet please follow the internet safety guidelines displayed on the Usborne Quicklinks Website. The websites recommended in Usborne Quicklinks are regularly reviewed. However, the content of a website may change at any time and Usborne Publishing is not responsible for the content of websites other than its own. We recommend that children are supervised while on the internet.

Usborne
Illustrated
Elementary
MATH
Dictionary

Kirsteen Rogers
and Tori Large

Designed by Karen Tomlins

Math consultant:
Sheila Ebbutt, BEAM Education

Illustrated by Ruth Russell

American editor: Carrie A. Armstrong
US consultant: Rhonda Bennett

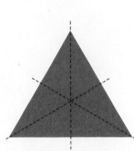
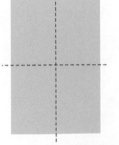

SCHOLASTIC INC.
New York Toronto London Auckland
Sydney Mexico City New Delhi Hong Kong

What is math?

Math is short for mathematics. It is the study of numbers, quantities and shapes. This book divides math into five main sections.

If you'd like to find out about a whole subject, you can turn to the section or pages and read straight through. If you just want to look up a particular word or fact, use the index at the back of the book to find out which page or pages to look at.

Numbers and number facts

Tells you about different kinds of numbers. It shows how they are the building blocks of mathematical calculations and tools you need for everyday life.

Calculations

Shows you lots of different ways to add, subtract, multiply and divide numbers: in your head, on paper, or using a calculator.

Shape and space

Gives you information about many shapes and solids, what makes them the way they are, and how you can change and move them in different ways.

Measurements

All about how to find out and describe how long, wide, tall and heavy things are, and how much containers of various shapes can hold. There's a useful section about time, too.

Dealing with data

Explains different ways you can collect and understand information, and shows you how to put it in graphs, charts and tables for other people to look at.

Contents

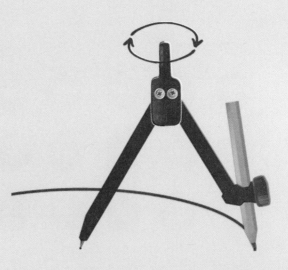

Numbers

Numbers help you count and describe all kinds of things. For example, you can use numbers to say how old you are, what time it is, how much things cost and how many muffins are on a plate.

Numerals

A numeral is a symbol or group of symbols you use to show a number. Each numeral below represents the number of buttons next to it.

0

1

Imagine how difficult it would be to describe how many buttons there are without using numerals.

2

3

4

5

6

7

8

9

Examples of numerals

Throughout history and across the world, people have used different numerals. Here are three ways of showing the number six:

These are Roman numerals, which were used in Ancient Rome. You sometimes see them carved on buildings to show the date.

VI

This is the Chinese numeral six. Chinese people say "liù."

六

Hindu-Arabic numerals are the numerals most people in the world use today.

6

Digits

A digit is any of the ten symbols 0 to 9. You can use digits together to make larger numbers. For example, you can use 3 and 4 to make numbers such as 34, 43 and 34,433.

The ten digits are:

0 1 2 3 4 5 6 7 8 9

Zero

Zero is the digit 0, which stands for no amount. You can use zero on its own, or with other digits to keep them in the right place within a number.

Without 0, the number 1,001 would become 11, which is a very different sized amount.

1,001

If zero didn't exist, you'd need to keep inventing new symbols to show big numbers. For example, in Roman numerals, which have no zero, 1,804 is written MDCCCIV.

In Roman numerals, M stands for 1,000, D stands for 500, C represents 100 and IV stands for 4.

1,804 MDCCCIV

Infinity

However big a number is, you can always add 1 to make a new, bigger number. And however small a number is, you can always subtract 1 to make a number that's even smaller. So numbers are infinite – they can go on forever.

This is the symbol for infinity.

Positive numbers

All numbers greater than zero are positive numbers. You can write them with or without a plus sign (+) in front, for example, +1 or 1. You can say either "plus one," "plus two," and so on, or usually just "one," "two," and so on.

These are examples of positive numbers.

0.5 1 24 356

Negative numbers

All numbers less than zero are negative numbers. A minus sign (–) in front tells you that a number is negative, for example, –1. You say "negative one" or "minus one," and so on.

These are examples of negative numbers.

−0.5 −1 −24 −356

The minus sign shows how many less than zero the number is. For example, –1 is 1 less than 0, and –24 is 24 less than 0. So –24 is smaller than –1.

Whole numbers or integers

Any numbers used for counting are called whole numbers or integers. They can be positive, negative or zero. Positive whole numbers are also called natural numbers.

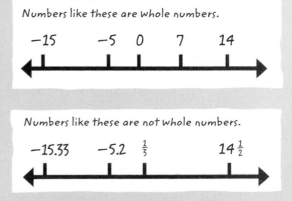

Numbers like these are whole numbers.

−15   −5   0   7   14

Numbers like these are not whole numbers.

−15.33   −5.2 $\frac{1}{3}$ $14\frac{1}{2}$

Find out more about: decimals (pages 21-24); fractions (pages 16-20); mixed numbers (page 17)

Number systems

A number system is a set of numbers and the rules you use for counting and doing calculations with them. The number system that you use in everyday counting is called the decimal system. It has ten digits: 0, 1, 2, 3, 4, 5, 6, 7, 8, 9. Another name for the decimal system is base ten.

Computers and other electronic things use a different number system, called base two or the binary system. This uses just two digits: 0 and 1.

Place value

Something's value is how much it is worth. A digit's place value is how much the digit is worth in a number. This depends where in the number the digit sits. For example, in the number 36, the digit 6 is in the ones (units) place, so it has a value of 6 ones. But in the number 630 it is in the hundreds place, so it is worth 6 hundreds.

The chart below shows different place values of the number 5. The zeros act as place holders, to show when there are no ones, no tens and so on.

Number lines

A number line is a picture of the numbers going on forever. Markings on the line are numbered in order of size.

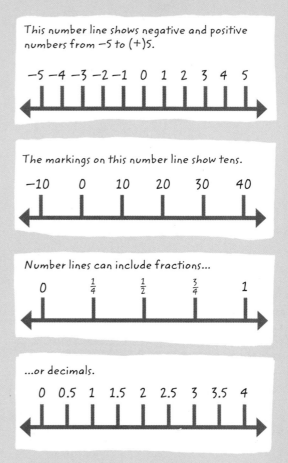

This number line shows negative and positive numbers from −5 to (+)5.

−5 −4 −3 −2 −1 0 1 2 3 4 5

The markings on this number line show tens.

−10 0 10 20 30 40

Number lines can include fractions...

0 $\frac{1}{4}$ $\frac{1}{2}$ $\frac{3}{4}$ 1

...or decimals.

0 0.5 1 1.5 2 2.5 3 3.5 4

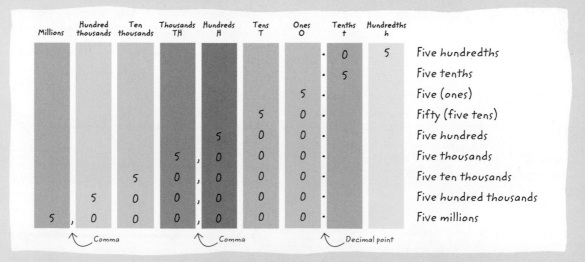

Millions	Hundred thousands	Ten thousands	Thousands TH	Hundreds H	Tens T	Ones O		Tenths t	Hundredths h	
							·	0	5	Five hundredths
							·	5		Five tenths
						5	·			Five (ones)
					5	0	·			Fifty (five tens)
				5	0	0	·			Five hundreds
			5 ,	0	0	0	·			Five thousands
		5	0 ,	0	0	0	·			Five ten thousands
	5	0	0 ,	0	0	0	·			Five hundred thousands
5 ,	0	0	0 ,	0	0	0	·			Five millions

↑ Comma   ↑ Comma   ↑ Decimal point

Find out more about: decimals (pages 21-24); **digits** (page 7); **fractions** (pages 16-20); **negative numbers** (page 7); **positive numbers** (page 7); **zero** (page 7)

Number relationships

Like people, all numbers have relationships, which help make them what they are. For example, you are you, but you are also a son or daughter, and a grandchild. It's the same with numbers too. For instance, 6 is 6; but it is also 3 sets of 2, 6 sets of 1, and half of 12.

Multiples

A multiple is the result you get when you multiply one whole number with another.

For example, some multiples of 3 are:

$$3 = (3 \times 1)$$
$$6 = (3 \times 2)$$
$$9 = (3 \times 3)$$

Common multiples

A number that's a multiple of two or more numbers is a common multiple. For example, 12 is a common multiple of 4 and 6. The lowest common multiple of two or more numbers is the smallest number that is a multiple of both.

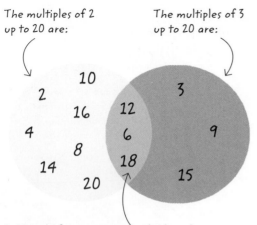

The multiples of 2 up to 20 are:

The multiples of 3 up to 20 are:

6, 12 and 18 are common multiples of these sets of numbers. 6 is the smallest of these, so 6 is the lowest common multiple of 2 and 3.

Even numbers

An even number is any multiple of 2. So all whole numbers that you can divide by 2 to give a whole number are even. An easy way to spot even numbers is to remember that they all end in 0, 2, 4, 6 or 8. (Zero itself is considered to be an even number.) So for example, 2, 48 and 556 are even numbers. This works for negative numbers as well, so –2, –48 and –556 are all even numbers too.

The first ten even numbers greater than zero are:

$$2 \quad 4 \quad 6 \quad 8 \quad 10$$
$$12 \quad 14 \quad 16 \quad 18 \quad 20$$

Odd numbers

Any number that's not a multiple of 2 is an odd number. So all whole numbers that you can't divide by 2 to give a whole number are odd. An easy way to spot odd numbers is to remember that they all end in 1, 3, 5, 7 or 9. So 5, 51 and 463 are all odd numbers. This works for negative numbers as well, so –5, –51 and –463 are all odd numbers too.

The first ten positive odd numbers are:

$$1 \quad 3 \quad 5 \quad 7 \quad 9$$
$$11 \quad 13 \quad 15 \quad 17 \quad 19$$

Find out more about: dividing (pages 46-61); **multiplying** (pages 46-59); **negative numbers** (page 7); **positive numbers** (page 7); **Venn diagrams** (page 121); **whole numbers** (page 7); **zero** (page 7)

Square numbers

When you multiply any number by itself you get a square number. For example, multiplying 4 by itself gives the square number 16.

The first ten square numbers are:

1   4   9   16   25

36   49   64   81   100

 You can show the square number 1 by a square measuring 1 x 1.

 You can show the square number 4 by a square measuring 2 x 2.

A block of squares measuring 3 x 3 shows the square number 9.

The square of an odd number is always odd and the square of an even number is always even. You can see this on the multiplication grid below.

This is a grid showing multiplications of numbers up to 10 x 10. The square numbers are in purple.

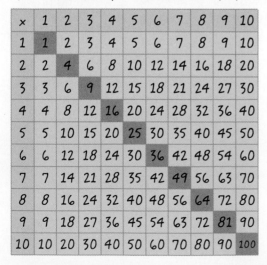

×	1	2	3	4	5	6	7	8	9	10
1	1	2	3	4	5	6	7	8	9	10
2	2	4	6	8	10	12	14	16	18	20
3	3	6	9	12	15	18	21	24	27	30
4	4	8	12	16	20	24	28	32	36	40
5	5	10	15	20	25	30	35	40	45	50
6	6	12	18	24	30	36	42	48	54	60
7	7	14	21	28	35	42	49	56	63	70
8	8	16	24	32	40	48	56	64	72	80
9	9	18	27	36	45	54	63	72	81	90
10	10	20	30	40	50	60	70	80	90	100

Powers

A power tells you to multiply a number by itself. (Another name for power is exponent.) The value of the power shows you how many sets of the number to multiply. For example, 4^3 means 4 to the power 3, which is 4 x 4 x 4. It is another way of writing 4 cubed, which is 64. This way of writing numbers is called index notation. Any number to the power 1, for example 3^1, is itself, so you don't usually write this power out.

Cube numbers

When you multiply any number by itself and then by itself again, you get a cube number. For example, multiplying 2 x 2 x 2 gives the cube number 8.

The first ten cube numbers are:

8   27   64   125   216   343

512   729   1,000

It's useful to remember that the cube of an odd number is always odd and the cube of an even number is always even.

You can show the cube number 1 by a cube measuring 1 x 1 x 1 units.

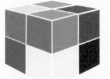 A cube measuring 2 x 2 x 2 units shows the cube number 8.

You can show the cube number 27 by a cube measuring 3 x 3 x 3 units.

Find out more about: even numbers (page 9); **multiplying** (pages 46-59); **odd numbers** (page 9)

Factors

A factor of a number is a whole number that divides exactly into it. For example, you can divide 12 exactly by 3 (to get 4), so 3 is a factor of 12.

The factors of 12 are:

$$1 \quad 2 \quad 3 \quad 4 \quad 6 \quad 12$$

You can divide 12 by any of these numbers to give a whole number:

$$12 \div 1 = 12$$
$$12 \div 2 = 6$$
$$12 \div 3 = 4$$
$$12 \div 4 = 3$$
$$12 \div 6 = 2$$
$$12 \div 12 = 1$$

You can write factors in pairs, and this is a good way to check that you have included them all. For example:

The factor pairs of 12 are:	This is because:
(1, 12)	$1 \times 12 = 12$
(2, 6)	$2 \times 6 = 12$
(3, 4)	$3 \times 4 = 12$

Factors of even numbers can be odd or even. But it's handy to remember that the factors of odd numbers are always odd numbers. You can divide every number by 1 and itself, so all numbers have at least two factors.

Factor tables

You can write the factors of numbers in a factor table. Some numbers have plenty of factors, but some have only two. The only number that has just one factor is 1. Square numbers have an odd number of factors.

This factor table shows the factors of the numbers up to 20. The numbers on yellow squares are square numbers.

Number	Factors
1	1
2	1, 2
3	1, 3
4	1, 2, 4
5	1, 5
6	1, 2, 3, 6
7	1, 7
8	1, 2, 4, 8
9	1, 3, 9
10	1, 2, 5, 10
11	1, 11
12	1, 2, 3, 4, 6, 12
13	1, 13
14	1, 2, 7, 14
15	1, 3, 5, 15
16	1, 2, 4, 8, 16
17	1, 17
18	1, 2, 3, 6, 9, 18
19	1, 19
20	1, 2, 4, 5, 10, 20

Find out more about: dividing (pages 46-61); **even numbers** (page 9); **odd numbers** (page 9); **whole numbers** (page 7)

Finding factors

To find all the factors of a number, first work out how many 1s are in it, then how many 2s, then 3s, and so on. Stop when a number repeats itself. For example:

To find the factors of 30:

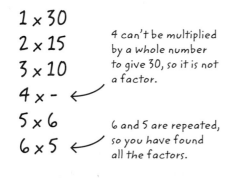

1×30

2×15

3×10 *4 can't be multiplied by a whole number to give 30, so it is not a factor.*

$4 \times -$

5×6 *6 and 5 are repeated, so you have found all the factors.*

6×5

The factors of 30 are 1, 2, 3, 5, 6, 10, 15 and 30.

Common factors

Common factors are numbers that divide exactly into two or more numbers to give a whole number. For example, the common, or same, factors of 9 and 12 are 1 and 3.

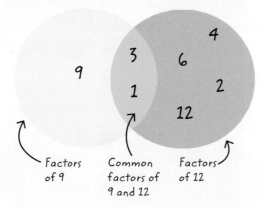

Factors of 9   Common factors of 9 and 12   Factors of 12

The greatest common factor (GCF) of 9 and 12 is 3, because it's the greatest number that is a factor of both of them.

Square roots

A square root is a factor of a number that you can multiply by itself to give that number. For example, the square root of 16 is 4. The symbol for square root is √.

$$4 \times 4 = 16$$
$$\text{So } \sqrt{16} = 4$$

Cube roots

A cube root is a factor of a number that you can multiply by itself twice to give that number. For example, the cube root of 8 is 2. The symbol for cube root is $\sqrt[3]{}$.

$$2 \times 2 \times 2 = 8$$
$$\text{So } \sqrt[3]{8} = 2$$

Perfect numbers

A perfect number is the sum of its factors (except for itself). For example:

6 is a perfect number because if you add its factors (except for itself), the answer is 6.

$$6 = 1 + 2 + 3$$

The next perfect number is 28.

$$28 = 1 + 2 + 4 + 7 + 14$$

Composite numbers

A composite number has three or more factors. For example, 10 has four factors: 1, 2, 5 and 10, so it is composite. Except for 2, all even numbers are composite. Every number greater than 1 is either a prime number or a composite number. You can find out about prime numbers on the next page.

Prime numbers

A number that you can only divide by 1 and itself is a prime number. Primes only have two factors.

The first ten positive prime numbers are:

2   3   5   7   11
13   17   19   23   29

To find out if a two-digit number is prime, try dividing it by 2, 3, 5 and 7. If these numbers are not factors, the number is prime. On the grid below, the numbers on green squares are multiples of 2, 3, 5 or 7. The numbers on purple squares are prime.

1	2	3	4	5	6	7	8	9	10
11	12	13	14	15	16	17	18	19	20
21	22	23	24	25	26	27	28	29	30
31	32	33	34	35	36	37	38	39	40
41	42	43	44	45	46	47	48	49	50
51	52	53	54	55	56	57	58	59	60
61	62	63	64	65	66	67	68	69	70
71	72	73	74	75	76	77	78	79	80
81	82	83	84	85	86	87	88	89	90
91	92	93	94	95	96	97	98	99	100

Here are some useful hints to remember about prime numbers:

• *1 is not a prime number because it only has one factor: 1.*
• *2 is the only even prime number. All the others are odd numbers.*
• *Except for 2 and 5, all prime numbers end in 1, 3, 7 or 9 (but not all numbers that end in 1, 3, 7 or 9 are prime).*

Prime factors

A factor that is also a prime number is called a prime factor. For example, the factors of 15 are 1, 3, 5 and 15. Of these, 3 and 5 are prime factors.

Factor trees

You can make a diagram called a factor tree to find out the prime factors of a number. To draw a factor tree for a number, take a pair of its factors and split each factor up into its own factor pairs, as shown below. Keep splitting the factors until you reach a factor that you can't divide any more, then draw a circle around it. These circled figures are the number's prime factors.

This is a factor tree for the number 60. You don't need to write down the factor pair 1 and 60, because 1 isn't a prime number, and it doesn't split 60 into any further factors.

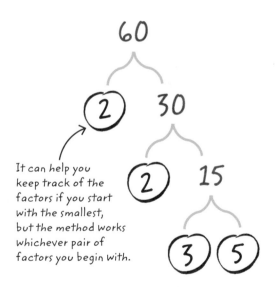

It can help you keep track of the factors if you start with the smallest, but the method works whichever pair of factors you begin with.

Once you have collected all the prime factors from the ends of the branches, you can write them out in order, starting with the smallest:

$$60 = 2 \times 2 \times 3 \times 5$$

Find out more about: dividing (pages 46-61); **even numbers** (page 9); **odd numbers** (page 9)

Sequences

A sequence is a set of things that are in order and follow a particular pattern or rule. For example, house numbers might follow a sequence of even numbers: 2, 4, 6, 8 and so on. Shapes and pictures can follow sequences too.

Terms

A term is any number, shape or picture in a sequence. For example:

1	2	4	8 ...
1st term	2nd term	3rd term	4th term

Each term in this number sequence is twice the term before it. The next term will be 16.

Dots at the end of a sequence means that it goes on forever.

The terms in this sequence are shapes. Each term has one more side than the one before it. The next term will be a shape with 6 sides.

These terms follow a color sequence. The next term will be a yellow marble.

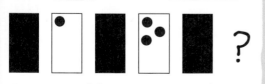

These pictures follow two sequences. The next term will be a white shape with 5 red spots on it.

Consecutive numbers

Whole numbers that are next to each other are called consecutive numbers. For example:

These numbers are consecutive:

1 2 3 4 5 6

So are these:

−21 −22 −23 −24 −25

These numbers are not consecutive:

−15 2 5 32 11 4

Rules

A rule is the pattern a sequence follows. You can often find the rule for working out the next term in a sequence by looking at the difference between the numbers. For example:

To find the rule for working out terms 6 and 7 in the sequence below, find the difference between each pair of numbers:

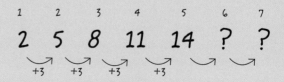

The rule is "add 3 each time," so the next two terms are 17 and 20.

Find out more about: even numbers (page 9); odd numbers (page 9); subtracting (pages 35-45); whole numbers (page 7)

Some common sequences

Sequence	First ten terms									
	1	2	3	4	5	6	7	8	9	10
Even numbers	2	4	6	8	10	12	14	16	18	20
Odd numbers	1	3	5	7	9	11	13	15	17	19
Square numbers	1	4	9	16	25	36	49	64	81	100
Cube numbers	1	8	27	64	125	216	343	512	729	1,000

Special sequences

Triangular numbers

If you add consecutive numbers from 1, you get triangular numbers. You can show them as triangular patterns of dots. The last row of dots gets one dot longer each time.

 $0 + 1 = 1$

 $0 + 1 + 2 = 3$

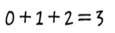 $0 + 1 + 2 + 3 = 6$

 $0 + 1 + 2 + 3 + 4 = 10$

 and so on.

The first ten triangular numbers are:

1 3 6 10 15

21 28 36 45 55

Fibonacci sequence

The first numbers in the Fibonacci sequence are 0 and 1. After that, you find each number by adding together the two terms before it. The sequence was named after Leonardo Fibonacci, who was an Italian mathematician. Numbers in the Fibonacci sequence are called Fibonacci numbers.

The Fibonacci sequence starts with 0 and 1. Here you can see how to work out the next few terms in the sequence.

0	$2 + 3 = 5$
1	$3 + 5 = 8$
$1 + 0 = 1$	$5 + 8 = 13$
$1 + 1 = 2$	$8 + 13 = 21$
$1 + 2 = 3$	and so on.

The first ten Fibonacci numbers are:

0 1 1 2 3 5 8

13 21 34

Find out more about: adding (pages 35-42); cube numbers (page 10); even numbers (page 9); odd numbers (page 9); square numbers (page 10)

Fractions

A fraction is a part of something. Fractions can be part of one thing, such as half an apple, or part of a group of things, for example, half of the apples on a tree.

Fraction notation

You can write fractions as one number on top of another. For example, a half is "one over two:" $\frac{1}{2}$. Writing fractions this way is called fraction notation. A few fractions have special names:

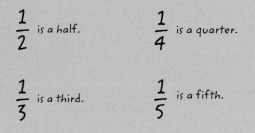

$\frac{1}{2}$ is a half. $\frac{1}{4}$ is a quarter.

$\frac{1}{3}$ is a third. $\frac{1}{5}$ is a fifth.

To say the names of most other fractions, add "th" to the name of the number, for example, sixth, seventh, and so on.

The top part of a fraction is called the numerator and the bottom part is the denominator. The denominator shows how many equal parts are in the whole amount and the numerator shows how many of them you're talking about.

$\frac{3}{4}$ *If you cut an apple into four equal pieces and eat three of them, you've eaten 3 out of 4 pieces. As a fraction this is $\frac{3}{4}$. The numerator is 3 and the denominator is 4.*

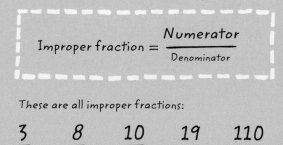

$\frac{3}{5}$ of these penguins have red scarves. $\frac{2}{5}$ of them have blue hats. $\frac{1}{5}$ of them has no winter wear.

Proper fractions

In a proper fraction the numerator is smaller than the denominator. Proper fractions are also called common fractions.

$$\text{Proper fraction} = \frac{\text{Numerator}}{\text{Denominator}}$$

These are all proper fractions:

$$\frac{1}{2} \qquad \frac{5}{6} \qquad \frac{2}{7} \qquad \frac{9}{13} \qquad \frac{99}{100}$$

Improper fractions

The numerator of an improper fraction is bigger than its denominator.

$$\text{Improper fraction} = \frac{\text{Numerator}}{\text{Denominator}}$$

These are all improper fractions:

$$\frac{3}{2} \qquad \frac{8}{6} \qquad \frac{10}{7} \qquad \frac{19}{13} \qquad \frac{110}{100}$$

Mixed numbers

A mixed number is made up of a whole number and a fraction.

Whole number → **2** $\frac{1}{3}$ ← Fraction

Changing a mixed number to an improper fraction

To change a mixed number to an improper fraction, multiply the whole number by the denominator and add the numerator. This gives you the new numerator; the denominator stays the same. For example:

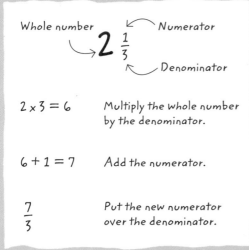

Whole number → **2** $\frac{1}{3}$ ← Numerator
← Denominator

$2 \times 3 = 6$ — Multiply the whole number by the denominator.

$6 + 1 = 7$ — Add the numerator.

$\frac{7}{3}$ — Put the new numerator over the denominator.

Changing an improper fraction to a mixed number

To change an improper fraction into a mixed number, divide the numerator by the denominator. For example:

$$\frac{9}{2} = 9 \div 2 = 4\frac{1}{2}$$

2 goes into 9 four times, with a half left over.

Equivalent fractions

Equivalent fractions are worth the same as each other, even though they look different. A fraction can have an infinite number of equivalent fractions. For example:

If you ate a part of this cake, you would get the same amount if you ate...

$\frac{1}{2}$ ...one half of the cake,

$\frac{2}{4}$ ...two quarters of the cake,

$\frac{3}{6}$ ...three sixths of the cake,

$\frac{4}{8}$ ...four eighths of the cake,

...and so on.

If the numerator and denominator are the same, the fraction is equivalent to a "whole one." Depending what you are looking at, this "whole one" might be the number 1, a whole thing, or a whole group of things.

$\frac{4}{4} = 1$

$\frac{6}{6}$ of this shape is equal to the whole shape.

$\frac{7}{7}$ of these butterflies are pink, so the whole group of butterflies is pink.

Find out more about: adding (pages 35–42); **dividing** (pages 46–61); **infinity** (page 7); **multiplying** (pages 46–59); **whole numbers** (page 7)

Finding equivalent fractions

You can see equivalent fractions on the fraction wall below. The "bricks" in each row add up to a whole. Look at bricks in other rows to see which fractions are the same as each other. For example:

This is a fraction (or equivalent fractions) wall. If you look down from $\frac{1}{2}$ you can see it's the same as two quarters, three sixths and four eighths.

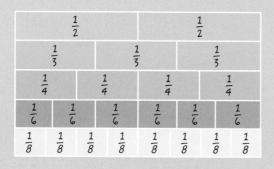

You can use the multiplication grid below to find equivalent fractions too. For example, to find fractions that are worth $\frac{1}{4}$, look along the "multiples of 1 row" (the row that starts with a 1) to find the numerator, and then along the "multiples of 4 row" (which starts with a 4) to find its related denominator.

On this multiplication grid, you can see that $\frac{2}{8}$, $\frac{3}{12}$ and $\frac{4}{16}$ are some equivalent fractions of $\frac{1}{4}$.

×	1	2	3	4	5	6	7	8	9	10
1	1	2	3	4	5	6	7	8	9	10
2	2	4	6	8	10	12	14	16	18	20
3	3	6	9	12	15	18	21	24	27	30
4	4	8	12	16	20	24	28	32	36	40
5	5	10	15	20	25	30	35	40	45	50
6	6	12	18	24	30	36	42	48	54	60
7	7	14	21	28	35	42	49	56	63	70
8	8	16	24	32	40	48	56	64	72	80
9	9	18	27	36	45	54	63	72	81	90
10	10	20	30	40	50	60	70	80	90	100

Calculating equivalent fractions

You can change a fraction into an equivalent fraction by multiplying or dividing the numerator and denominator by the same number.

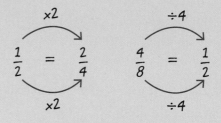

Simplifying fractions

To simplify a fraction, divide the numerator and the denominator by the same number. This gives you an equivalent fraction that uses smaller numbers. Sometimes this is called canceling fractions. Eventually you can't divide the numerator and the denominator any more. This means the fraction is in its simplest form or lowest terms.

For example, to find the simplest form of $\frac{6}{12}$:

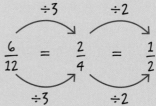

Remember, you can't divide 1 by any more whole numbers, so when either the numerator or denominator is 1, the fraction is in its simplest form.

To find the simplest form of $\frac{8}{12}$:

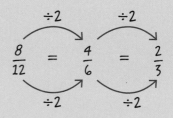

2 and 3 don't have any common factors, so the fraction is in its simplest form.

Find out more about: adding (pages 35-42); **common factors** (page 12); **denominators** (page 16); **dividing** (pages 46-61); **equivalent fractions** (page 17); **multiples** (page 9); **multiplying** (pages 46-59); **numerators** (page 16)

Equivalence strips

You can compare simple fractions by making equivalence strips. Cut paper strips the same length as each other (one strip for each fraction). For each fraction, divide a strip into the number of equal parts shown by the denominator and color the number of parts shown by the numerator. Then compare the length of the colored parts.

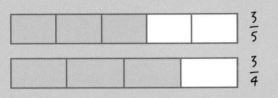

$\frac{3}{5}$

$\frac{3}{4}$

These equivalence strips show that $\frac{3}{4}$ is bigger than $\frac{3}{5}$.

Common denominators

You can compare fractions by writing them over their lowest common denominator. This is the lowest number that is a multiple of both denominators. For example:

To compare $\frac{1}{8}$, $\frac{3}{4}$ and $\frac{1}{2}$, rewrite them as equivalent fractions over their lowest common denominator, which is 8:

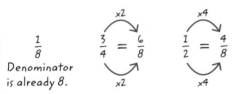

$\frac{1}{8}$

Denominator is already 8.

$\frac{3}{4} = \frac{6}{8}$

$\frac{1}{2} = \frac{4}{8}$

You can now compare the fractions and see that $\frac{6}{8}$ is the biggest, so $\frac{3}{4}$ is the largest fraction in the original list.

Fractions on a number line

You can write fractions on a number line. For example:

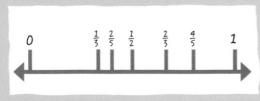

Fractions of quantities

To find a fraction of a quantity or amount, you need to divide the total amount by the denominator. Then multiply the result by the numerator.

For example, $\frac{2}{3}$ of the chocolates in a box have toffee fillings. To find out how many toffees there are:

$\frac{2}{3}$ of 30

$30 \div 3 = 10$ Divide 30 by the denominator (3).

$10 \times 2 = 20$ Multiply the result by the numerator (2).

There are 20 toffees in the box.

Calculator tips

Some calculators have a fraction key like this: $\boxed{A^B/c}$. To type in a proper fraction, type in the numerator, press $\boxed{A^B/c}$, then type in the denominator.

For example to type $\frac{2}{3}$, press $\boxed{2}\ \boxed{A^B/c}\ \boxed{3}$. You type in mixed numbers in a similar way. For example, to type $1\frac{2}{3}$, press $\boxed{1}\ \boxed{A^B/c}\ \boxed{2}\ \boxed{A^B/c}\ \boxed{3}$.

If your calculator doesn't have a fraction key, you can use the $\boxed{\div}$ key to type in fractions instead.

For example, to key in $\frac{2}{3}$, press $\boxed{2}\ \boxed{\div}\ \boxed{3}$. Remember to change mixed fractions to improper fractions before you type them in.

To add, subtract, multiply and divide fractions on your calculator, type in a fraction, then press the $\boxed{+}$, $\boxed{-}$, $\boxed{x}$ or $\boxed{\div}$ button. Put in the next fraction and press $\boxed{=}$.

Find out more about: denominators (page 16); **dividing** (pages 46-61); **multiples** (page 9); **multiplying** (pages 46-59); **number lines** (page 8); **numerators** (page 16)

Adding fractions

Change any whole or mixed numbers into improper fractions. If the fractions you want to add have different denominators, you'll need to rewrite them over a common denominator. Then add together the numerators and cancel down your answer to its simplest form.

$$1\frac{2}{3} + \frac{1}{2}$$

$$= \frac{5}{3} + \frac{1}{2}$$ Change the mixed number to an improper fraction.

$$= \frac{10}{6} + \frac{3}{6}$$ Rewrite the fractions over a common denominator (here, 6).

$$= \frac{13}{6}$$ Add the numerators.

$$= 2\frac{1}{6}$$ Write the fraction in its simplest form.

Multiplying fractions

Change any whole or mixed numbers into improper fractions. Multiply the numerators then multiply the denominators. Then cancel down your answer to its simplest form.

$$2\frac{2}{3} \times \frac{1}{2}$$

$$= \frac{8}{3} \times \frac{1}{2}$$ Change the mixed number to an improper fraction.

$$= \frac{8 \times 1}{3 \times 2}$$ Multiply the numerators. Multiply the denominators.

$$= \frac{8}{6}$$

$$= 1\frac{2}{6}$$

$$= 1\frac{1}{3}$$ Write the fraction in its simplest form.

Subtracting fractions

Change any whole or mixed numbers into improper fractions. If the denominators are different, rewrite the fractions over a common denominator. Subtract the second numerator from the first, then cancel down your answer to its simplest form.

$$1\frac{2}{3} - \frac{1}{2}$$

$$= \frac{5}{3} - \frac{1}{2}$$ Change the mixed number to an improper fraction.

$$= \frac{10}{6} - \frac{3}{6}$$ Rewrite the fractions over a common denominator (here, 6).

$$= \frac{7}{6}$$ Subtract the second numerator from the first.

$$= 1\frac{1}{6}$$ Write the fraction in its simplest form.

Dividing fractions

Change any whole or mixed numbers into improper fractions. Turn the second fraction upside down and multiply the fractions together (see above). Then cancel down your answer to its simplest form.

$$2\frac{2}{3} \div \frac{1}{2}$$

$$= \frac{8}{3} \div \frac{1}{2}$$ Change the mixed number to an improper fraction.

$$= \frac{8}{3} \times \frac{2}{1}$$ Turn the second fraction upside down and multiply.

$$= \frac{8 \times 2}{3 \times 1}$$ Multiply the numerators. Multiply the denominators.

$$= \frac{16}{3}$$

$$= 5\frac{1}{3}$$ Write the fraction in its simplest form.

Find out more about: canceling fractions (page 18); **common denominators** (page 19); **denominators, improper fractions** (page 16); **mixed numbers** (page 17); **numerators** (page 16); **simplest form** (page 18); **whole numbers** (page 7)

Decimals

A decimal is made up of whole numbers and parts of whole numbers, separated by a dot called a decimal point. 0.1, 22.3 and −12.119 are all examples of decimals. Digits after the decimal point represent fractions that are tenths, hundredths and thousandths.

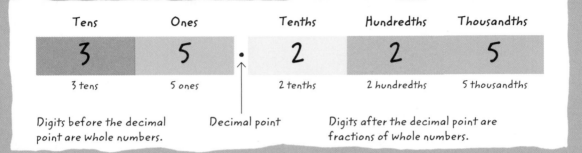

Tens	Ones		Tenths	Hundredths	Thousandths
3	5	.	2	2	5
3 tens	5 ones		2 tenths	2 hundredths	5 thousandths

Digits before the decimal point are whole numbers.

Decimal point

Digits after the decimal point are fractions of whole numbers.

Decimal fractions

A decimal fraction is a decimal number that is less than 1. For example, 0.25 is a decimal fraction.

0.25 stands for $0 + \dfrac{2}{10} + \dfrac{5}{100}$

0.126 stands for

$0 + \dfrac{1}{10} + \dfrac{2}{100} + \dfrac{6}{1,000}$

Mixed decimals

A decimal number that is more than 1, for example, 7.13, is called a mixed decimal.

7.13 stands for $7 + \dfrac{1}{10} + \dfrac{3}{100}$

19.296 stands for

$19 + \dfrac{2}{10} + \dfrac{9}{100} + \dfrac{6}{1,000}$

Both decimal fractions and mixed decimals are often just called decimals.

Recurring decimals

A decimal that has digits that repeat infinitely (endlessly) is called a recurring decimal. For example, 1 ÷ 3 gives the recurring decimal 0.333333... A recurring decimal can be written with a line over the recurring digit, like this: $0.\overline{3}$

You might sometimes see decimals with repeating groups of digits in them, for example 0.125 125 125 125... They are written with a line over the first and last digit in the recurring group: $0.\overline{125}$

This decimal is recurring – its digits repeat forever.

0.3333333

Find out more about: **digits** (page 7); **fractions** (pages 16-20); **infinity** (page 7); **whole numbers** (page 7)

Decimal places

A digit's position after the decimal point is its decimal place (d.p. for short). You usually see decimals written with 1, 2 or 3 digits after the decimal point. They are written to 1, 2, or 3 decimal places.

3.2   1 decimal place (1 d.p.)

3.24   2 decimal places (2 d.p.)

3.246   3 decimal places (3 d.p.)

Putting a zero on the end of a decimal number doesn't change its value. For example, 5.25 (2 d.p.) is worth the same as 5.250 (3 d.p.) or 5.2500 (4 d.p.). You can find out more about using decimals and decimal places on pages 32 and 33.

Decimals and fractions

Some fractions and decimals are used more often than others. Here's a list of common ones to look for:

$$\frac{1}{2} = 0.5 \qquad \frac{1}{10} = 0.1$$

$$\frac{1}{4} = 0.25 \qquad \frac{1}{100} = 0.01$$

$$\frac{3}{4} = 0.75 \qquad \frac{1}{3} = 0.\overline{3}$$

$$\frac{1}{5} = 0.2 \qquad \frac{2}{3} = 0.\overline{6}$$

$$\frac{1}{8} = 0.125$$

$\frac{1}{3}$ and $\frac{2}{3}$ form recurring decimal fractions.

Gattegno charts

A Gattegno chart shows how the decimal place of a digit affects its value.

If you look down each column of the chart you can see that when a digit moves one decimal place to the left, its value becomes 10 times bigger. For example, 0.3 is worth 10 times more than 0.03, and 8 is 10 times bigger than 0.8.

Thousandths	0.001	0.002	0.003	0.004	0.005	0.006	0.007	0.008	0.009
Hundredths	0.01	0.02	0.03	0.04	0.05	0.06	0.07	0.08	0.09
Tenths	0.1	0.2	0.3	0.4	0.5	0.6	0.7	0.8	0.9
Ones	1	2	3	4	5	6	7	8	9
Tens	10	20	30	40	50	60	70	80	90
Hundreds	100	200	300	400	500	600	700	800	900

If you read from the bottom of a column upward, you can see that as the digit moves one decimal place to the right, its value becomes 10 times smaller. For example, this means that 0.03 is worth 10 times less than 0.3, and 0.8 is 10 times smaller than 8.

Find out more about: decimal point (page 21); **decimals** (pages 21-24); **digits** (page 7); **fractions** (pages 16-20); **place value** (page 8); **recurring decimals** (page 21); **zero** (page 7)

Changing decimals to fractions

You can change a decimal to a fraction by writing it as tenths, hundredths, thousandths or so on. If possible, cancel each fraction to its simplest form.

If a decimal has 1 decimal place, write it as tenths, then simplify it if you can. For example:

0.6 is 6 tenths

$$= \frac{6}{10}$$

Cancel it to its simplest form (here, by dividing the numerator and denominator by 2).

$$= \frac{3}{5}$$

If a decimal has 2 decimal places, write it as hundredths then, if it's possible, simplify it. For example:

0.65 is 65 hundredths

$$= \frac{65}{100}$$

Cancel it to its simplest form (here, by dividing the numerator and denominator by 5).

$$= \frac{13}{20}$$

If a decimal has 3 decimal places, write it as thousandths, then simplify it if you can. For example:

0.875 is 875 thousandths

$$= \frac{875}{1,000}$$

$$= \frac{175}{200}$$

Cancel it to its simplest form (here, by dividing the numerator and denominator by 5, three times).

$$= \frac{35}{40}$$

$$= \frac{7}{8}$$

Changing fractions to decimals

It's easy to change a fraction to a decimal using your calculator: just divide the numerator by the denominator, and the result is your answer.

You can change fractions to decimals without a calculator, too, by multiplying the fraction by 1.00. When you change a common fraction to a decimal, the number will always be less than 1. For example, to change $\frac{2}{5}$ to a decimal:

$$\frac{2}{5} \times 1.00$$

Multiply by 1.00.

$$= \frac{2 \times 1.00}{5 \times 1}$$

You may find it helps to rewrite 1.00 as $\frac{1.00}{1}$.

$$= \frac{2.00}{5}$$

Divide the numerator by the denominator.

$$= 0.40$$

$$= 0.4$$

The last 0 is not needed so you can write the decimal without it.

If you change a mixed number to a decimal, the number will always be more than 1. First of all, change the fraction part to a decimal, then add the whole number. For example, to change $2\frac{3}{8}$ to a decimal:

$$2\frac{3}{8} \times 1.00$$

$$= 2 + \left(\frac{3}{8} \times 1.00\right)$$

Parentheses ( ) tell you which part of a calculation to do first. You may find it helps to rewrite 1.00 as $\frac{1.00}{1}$.

$$= 2 + \left(\frac{3 \times 1.00}{8 \times 1}\right)$$

$$= 2 + \left(\frac{3.00}{8}\right)$$

Change the fraction to a decimal first, then add on the whole number.

$$= 2 + 0.375$$

$$= 2.375$$

Find out more about: common fractions (page 16); **denominators** (page 16); **dividing** (pages 46-61); **fractions** (pages 16-20); **mixed numbers** (page 17); **numerators** (page 16); **simplifying fractions** (page 18)

Adding decimals

You can add up decimals without a calculator too. Write the numbers down like this, with the decimal points lined up. Then add the digits in each column, starting at the right-hand side.

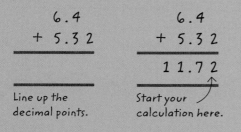

```
  6 . 4          6 . 4
+ 5 . 3 2      + 5 . 3 2
_____      _____
               1 1 . 7 2
_____
```

Line up the   Start your
decimal points.   calculation here.

Subtracting decimals

To subtract decimals without a calculator, write down the numbers like this, with the decimal points lined up. Then subtract the bottom digit in each column from the one above, starting at the right.

```
  3 . 8          3 . 8
- 2 . 4        - 2 . 4
_____      _____
                 1 . 4
_____
```

Line up the   Start your
decimal points.   calculation here.

Multiplying decimals

To multiply decimals without a calculator, ignore the decimal point and multiply both numbers as if they were whole numbers. Then put in the decimal point: the number of decimal places in the answer is the same as the total number of decimal places in the question.

For example, to multiply 3.6 by 0.5, use 36 × 5.

```
        3 6
    ×   5
    _____
    1 8 0
```

So 3.6 × 0.5 = 1.80
(1 d.p.) + (1 d.p.) = (2 d.p.)

Dividing decimals

To divide decimals without using a calculator, multiply both numbers by 10, 100 or 1,000 (or a higher power of 10 if needed) to change them into whole numbers. Now do the division as normal – your answer will be the same as if you had divided the decimals.

For example, to divide 2.5 by 0.5, multiply both numbers by 10 and use 25 ÷ 5.

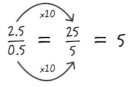

$$\frac{2.5}{0.5} = \frac{25}{5} = 5$$

To decide which power of 10 to multiply the numbers by, look at the decimal that has the most digits after the decimal point. If it has 1 decimal place, multiply both numbers by 10 or if it has 2 decimal places, multiply them by 100. Multiply by 1,000 if it has 3 decimal places, and so on.

Percentages

A percentage is a special fraction with a denominator of 100. Percent means parts for each 100. You write percentages using the symbol %. For example, 20 percent (20%) means 20 parts for each 100, $\frac{20}{100}$ or 20 hundredths.

This symbol is used to show percentages.

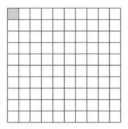

There are 100 squares on this grid. 1 is blue, so you can say that 1% of the squares is blue.

Finding percentages of shapes

To find a percentage of a shape, first count all the equal parts. Then divide 100 by this number, to find out what percentage each part is worth. Multiply the result by the number of parts you need. For example:

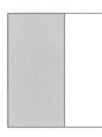

$\frac{1}{4}$ of the shape is blue, so 25% of it is blue.

This shape has 10 equal parts, so each part is 10% (100 ÷ 10). 3 parts are orange, so 30% (3 x 10%) of the shape is orange. 70% (7 x 10%) of the shape is green.

$\frac{1}{2}$ of the shape is blue, so 50% of it is blue.

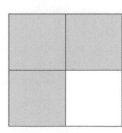

$\frac{3}{4}$ of the shape is blue, so 75% of it is blue.

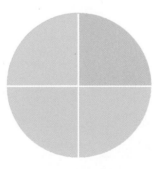

This shape is divided into 4 equal parts, so each part is 25% (100 ÷ 4). 1 part is orange, so 25% of the shape is orange. 75% (3 x 25%) of it is green.

Finding percentages of quantities

You can use different ways to find the percentage of a quantity.

The 10% method

This method is ideal if you want to find a percentage that's a multiple of 10%, for example 20%. First, divide the number of objects by 10. This tells you how many objects are 10% of the total. Then multiply your answer by the number of 10%s you need.

For example, a store has 40 cans of paint and 20% of them are red. To find out how many cans of red paint there are:

Find 10% of 40:

$40 \div 10 = 4$

Find how many sets of 10% you need:

$20\% = 2 \times 10\%$

so 20% of 40

$= 2 \times 4 = 8$

There are 8 cans of red paint.

You can also use this method to help you calculate percentages that end in 5, 2.5 or 7.5, such as 15%, 17.5% or 22.5%. For example, if 17.5% of the 40 cans in the store are blue:

10% of 40 = 4

so

5% of 40 = 2

2.5% of 40 = 1

17.5% = 10% + 5% + 2.5%

so 17.5% of 40

$= 4 + 2 + 1 = 7$

There are 7 cans of blue paint.

Using fractions

Change the percentage into a fraction, by writing it over a denominator of 100. Next, change the total number of objects into a fraction by writing it over a denominator of 1. Then multiply the fractions and write the answer in its simplest form. For example, if 30% of 40 cans of paint are yellow, you could find out how many are yellow by:

$$\frac{30}{100} \times 40 = \frac{30 \times 40}{100 \times 1} = \frac{1{,}200}{100} = 12$$

There are 12 cans of yellow paint.

Using decimals

Change the percentage into a decimal, by taking off the percentage sign and dividing the number by 100. Then multiply the decimal by the total number of objects to find the answer. For example, if 20% of 40 cans of paint are green, you could find out how many cans of green paint there are by:

20% is 0.2

$$0.2 \times 40 = 8$$

There are 8 cans of green paint.

5 of these 40 cans of paint are white, which is the same as 12.5%.

 Find out more about: decimals (pages 21-24); denominators (page 16); dividing (pages 46-61); fractions (pages 16-20); multiples (page 9); multiplying (pages 46-59); place value (page 8); powers (page 10); simplifying fractions (page 18)

Changing...
...decimals to percentages
Multiply the decimal by 100 and add a percentage sign. For example, to change 0.68 to a percentage:

$$0.68 \times 100 = 68\%$$

...percentages to decimals
Take off the percentage sign and divide the percentage by 100. For example, to change 15% to a decimal:

$$15 \div 100 = 0.15$$

...fractions to percentages
Multiply the fraction by 100 (it may help you to rewrite it as $\frac{100}{1}$). Simplify it if you can and add a percentage sign. For example, to change $\frac{3}{4}$ to a percentage:

$$\frac{3}{4} \times 100$$

$$= \frac{3 \times 100}{4 \times 1} = \frac{300}{4}$$

$$= 75\%$$

...percentages to fractions
Take off the percentage sign and write the number as a fraction, with a denominator of 100. Simplify it if you can. For example, to change 45% to a fraction:

$$\frac{45}{100}$$ Write it over a denominator of 100.

$$= \frac{9}{20}$$ (Divide by 5 to simplify to its lowest terms.)

Equivalent values
Percentages, fractions and decimals are different ways of writing the same numbers. Here are some percentages and their equivalent fractions and decimals. It's useful to recognize them and understand how to work them out.

Fraction → $\frac{Numerator \div}{Denominator}$ → Decimal

Decimal → Decimal x 100 → Percentage

Fraction		Decimal		Percentage
$\frac{3}{4}$	=	0.75	=	75%
$\frac{1}{2}$	=	0.5	=	50%
$\frac{1}{4}$	=	0.25	=	25%
$\frac{1}{5}$	=	0.2	=	20%
$\frac{1}{10}$	=	0.1	=	10%
$\frac{1}{20}$	=	0.05	=	5%
$\frac{1}{100}$	=	0.01	=	1%

Calculator tips
You can use the fraction and decimal methods on your calculator to find percentages of quantities. (Remember to estimate and check your results.)

For example, to use the fraction method to find 5% of 40, key in:

`5 ÷ 1 0 0 x 4 0 =`

To use the decimal method to do the same calculation, key in:

`0 . 0 5 x 4 0 =`

Find out more about: decimals (pages 21-24); denominators (page 16); dividing (pages 46-61); estimating (page 34); fractions (pages 16-20); multiplying (pages 46-59); simplifying fractions (page 18); whole numbers (page 7)

Sale prices and discounts

In a sale, stores sell items at lower prices. Sale prices and discounts are often shown as percentages, for example "10% off." To find the new price, work out the value of the percentage, then subtract that amount from the full price. For example:

A clothing store has a 20% sale. If a coat usually costs $55, you can find out its sale price by:

$$\frac{20}{100} \times \$55 = \frac{1}{5} \times \$55 = \$11$$

This is the discount.

$$\$55 - \$11 = \$44$$

Old cost − Discount = New cost

The sale price of the coat is $44.

To use a calculator to work this out, key in:

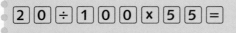

then:

$$\boxed{5}\,\boxed{5}\,\boxed{-}\,\boxed{1}\,\boxed{1}\,\boxed{=}$$

Percentage increases

When the price or size of something gets bigger by a percentage, the change is called a percentage increase. To work out the new price or size, you need to calculate the value of the percentage and add it to the original amount. For example:

An auto shop increases its prices by 5%. If a service usually costs $260, you can find out its new price by:

$$\frac{5}{100} \times \$260 = \frac{1}{20} \times \$260 = \$13$$

This is the increase.

$$\$260 + \$13 = \$273$$

Old cost + Increase = New cost

The new cost of a service is $273.

To use a calculator to work this out, key in:

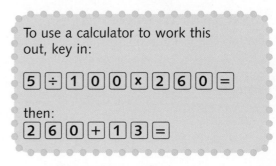

then:

$$\boxed{2}\,\boxed{6}\,\boxed{0}\,\boxed{+}\,\boxed{1}\,\boxed{3}\,\boxed{=}$$

One quantity as a percentage of another

You can find out what percentage one quantity is of another by making the quantities into a fraction and multiplying it by 100%. For example, if 42 out of 60 children prefer apple juice over orange juice, you could find out what percentage prefer apple juice by:

$$\frac{42}{60} \times 100\%$$

Simplify the fraction if you can.

$$\frac{7}{10} \times 100\% = \frac{700}{10}\% = 70\%$$

70% of the children prefer apple juice over orange juice.

If you use a calculator to work this out, you can skip the simplifying stage and just key in:

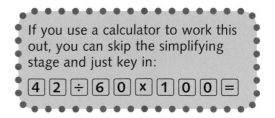

Proportion and ratio

Proportion and ratio are ways of comparing quantities. They are closely linked to fractions, so it's a good idea to make sure you understand those first.

Proportion

Proportion compares a part of something with the whole thing. It is the same as finding a fraction of a whole amount. For example, there are 5 fish in the bowl on the right, and 3 are orange. The proportion of orange fish is 3 in 5, or $\frac{3}{5}$.

Ratios

Ratio compares one amount with another. For example, there are 3 orange fish to 2 purple fish in the bowl, so the ratio of orange fish to purple ones is 3 to 2. You write this as 3:2. It's useful to think of the two dots as meaning "compared to."

You can have ratios in continuous quantities too. For example, the directions on a drink mix might tell you to mix 1 part powder to 4 parts water. So whatever size drink you prepare, you will always need 4 times as much water as powder.

Simplifying ratios

To simplify a ratio, divide both sides by the same number, to give an equivalent ratio that uses smaller whole numbers. When you can't divide the numbers any more, the ratio is in its simplest form or lowest terms. For example:

The ratio of yellow to purple stars is 2:6. By dividing each number by 2, you can simplify this ratio to 1:3.

Direct proportion

When two amounts are in direct proportion, and one amount gets bigger or smaller, the other amount will also get bigger or smaller by the same ratio. For example, if the ratio of orange to purple fish is 3:2, and you double the number of orange fish, you will need to double the number of purple fish too. The ratio 6:4 is an equivalent ratio of 3:2.

To solve direct proportion problems, write the numbers in a chart like this, and see how the pattern of numbers continues.

Orange fish	Purple fish
3	2
6	4
9	6
12	?

Here, the purple fish numbers are going up in 2s. So if you had 12 orange fish, you would also have 8 purple fish (6 + 2).

Find out more about: fractions (pages 16-20); **whole numbers** (page 7)

Unit amounts

A unit amount is what one part of a thing is worth. For example, the unit amount in a pack of yogurts is the price of one container of yogurt. If a store sells packs of yogurts in two sizes, you can use unit amounts to find out which pack is better value.

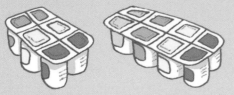

Pack A: 6 for $2.40   Pack B: 8 for $2.80

The unit amount (the cost of each container) in pack A is:

$$\$2.40 \div 6 = \$0.40$$

The unit amount (the cost of each container) in pack B is:

$$\$2.80 \div 8 = \$0.35$$

Each yogurt in pack B costs less, so pack B is the better value.

If 4 oranges cost $1.00, how much will 14 oranges cost?

The unit amount (the cost of 1 orange) is:

$$\$1.00 \div 4 = \$0.25$$

The cost of 14 oranges is:

$$14 \times \$0.25 = \$3.50$$

Rational numbers

Any number you can show as the ratio of two whole numbers is a rational number. All fractions and whole numbers are rational, as well as all decimal fractions that don't go on forever. For example, $\frac{2}{3}$, −6 and 0.531 are rational numbers because you can show them as the ratios 2:3, −6:1 and 531:1,000.

Sharing an amount in a ratio

To divide an amount in a particular ratio, first add up the parts in the ratio to find the total number of parts. Next, divide the amount by this total to find the unit amount. Then multiply the unit amount by each part of the ratio in turn.

For example, if Mabel and Martha divide 50 beads between them in the ratio 3:2, you can find out how many beads each girl has by:

$3 + 2 = 5$ parts
5 parts $= 50$ beads
1 part $= 50 \div 5 = 10$ beads

Mabel has 3 parts:
$3 \times 10 = 30$ beads

Martha has 2 parts:
$2 \times 10 = 20$ beads

It is a good idea to check that your answers add up to the original number.
$(30 + 20 = 50)$

If the girls share the beads with Sam in the ratio 5:3:2:

$5 + 3 + 2 = 10$ parts
10 parts $= 50$ beads
1 part $= 50 \div 10 = 5$ beads

Mabel has 5 parts:
$5 \times 5 = 25$ beads

Martha has 3 parts:
$3 \times 5 = 15$ beads

Sam has 2 parts:
$2 \times 5 = 10$ beads

Check your answer:
$(25 + 15 + 10 = 50)$

 Find out more about: decimal fractions (page 21); fractions (pages 16-20); multiplying (46-59); ratios (page 29); recurring decimals (page 21); whole numbers (page 7)

Comparing numbers

It's very useful to be able to compare numbers and quantities, to find out whether one is bigger, smaller or if they're the same size. For example, you could compare prices in a store, scores in a game, or the length of a TV program with the time left before bed.

Significant figures

Significant figures are the digits in a number as you read them from left to right. For example, the first significant figure in 4,213 is 4, then 2, then 1, then 3.

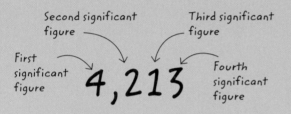

You can round 4,213 to three significant figures (4,210), two significant figures (4,200), or one significant figure (4,000).

Comparison signs

Here are some useful symbols that show the relationship between two numbers:

 means "less than."
For example, 4 < 10
means 4 is less than 10.

> means "greater than."
For example, 15 > 10
means 15 is greater than 10.

The widest part of the > and < signs always points to the larger number.

= means "equal to."
For example, 2 + 3 = 5
means 2 + 3 is equal to 5.

Comparing whole numbers

You can find out if numbers are bigger or smaller than others by comparing the place value of their significant figures.

An easy way to compare whole numbers is to write them under each other, lining up the digits in the ones column. For example, the top five scores on a computer game are 73, 115, 1,560, 69 and 677. To compare them, first list them with the ones digits lined up:

Thousands	Hundreds	Tens	Ones
		7	3
	1	1	5
1	5	6	0
		6	9
	6	7	7

Now you can compare the numbers by looking at the thousands, hundreds, tens and ones, reading them from the left.

You can see that 1,560 is the highest score, because it is the only number with thousands in it. 69 and 73 are the shortest numbers, but 60 is lower than 70, which means 69 is smaller than 73, so 69 is the lowest score in this list.

Find out more about: **place value** (page 8); **rounding** (page 33); **whole numbers** (page 7)

Comparing decimals

To compare decimals, first list them one above the other, with the decimal points lined up. You might find it easier to compare the numbers if you write them out with the same number of digits after the decimal point. (You can do this by writing 0s on the end of numbers with fewer decimal places). Then, starting at the left, compare the place value of the significant figures. For example, to find out which of these packages is lightest:

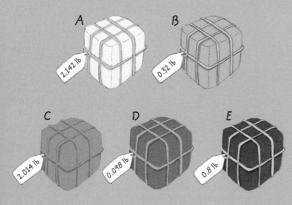

	Ones		Tenths	Hundredths	Thousandths
A	2	.	1	4	2
B	0	.	3	2	0
C	2	.	0	1	4
D	0	.	0	9	8
E	0	.	8	0	0

Write in 0s to fill empty decimal places.

You can now compare the weights by looking at the whole numbers, then the decimal places, reading from left to right. In this case, package D is the lightest. Although it contains high digits (9 and 8), they have low place values, and the number has no ones or tenths.

Comparing mixed numbers

If you need to compare a mixture of fractions, decimals and percentages, change them into decimals first, then treat them like ordinary decimals.

Ordering numbers

Once you have compared numbers, you can put them in order.

Ascending order

A list of numbers that goes up, or increases, in value is in ascending order. For example:

The value gets bigger.

69
73
115
677
1,560

These scores are in ascending order.

The value gets bigger.

0.098 lb
0.32 lb
0.8 lb
2.014 lb
2.142 lb

These weights are in ascending order.

Descending order

A list of numbers that goes down, or decreases, in value is in descending order. For example:

The value gets smaller.

1,560
677
115
73
69

These scores are in descending order.

The value gets smaller.

2.142 lb
2.014 lb
0.8 lb
0.32 lb
0.098 lb

These weights are in descending order.

Find out more about: decimal point (page 21); **decimals** (pages 21-24); **digits** (page 7); **fractions** (pages 16-20); **pounds** (page 102); **percentages** (pages 25-28); **place value** (page 8); **weight** (page 102)

Rounding

Rounding means giving a number a nearby value. You might do this if you don't need an exact number, or to make numbers that are easier to remember, or easier to use.

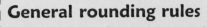
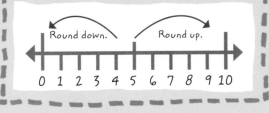
Deciding what to round to

What you round to often depends on what the number is describing. For example, you might round a plant's height to the nearest inch, but a country's population to the nearest hundred thousand people.

Rounding to the nearest 10

To round a number to the nearest 10, look at the digit in the ones column and follow the rounding rules. For example:

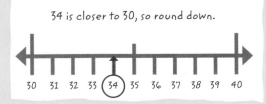

Rounding to the nearest 100

To round a number to the nearest 100, look at the digit in the tens column and follow the rounding rules. For example:

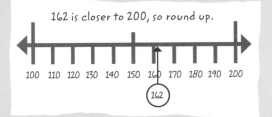

Rounding to the nearest 1,000

To round a number to the nearest 1,000, look at the digit in the hundreds column and follow the rounding rules. For example:

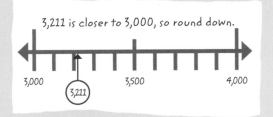

Rounding to 3 s.f. or 2 d.p.

Math questions often ask you to round your answers to 3 significant figures (3 s.f.) or 2 decimal places (2 d.p.). Always write down the rounding you have done, for example 3.75 (2 d.p.) or 851 (3 s.f.).

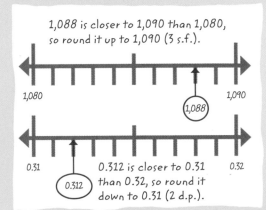

Find out more about: **decimal places** (page 22); **digits** (page 7); **significant figures** (page 31)

Estimating and calculating

Before you start doing a calculation to work out an exact answer to a question, it's a good idea to estimate the answer. This means using the information you have to make a rough or approximate guess. You can then tell if your exact answer is a sensible one.

Estimating quantities

A good way to estimate a number of things without counting every single one is to divide them roughly into groups. You can then count the number of things in one group and multiply your answer by the number of groups. For example, to estimate the number of flowers in the pots, you could try counting the flowers in one pot and multiplying by the number of pots.

There are approximately 60 flowers.

Approximation sign

$\approx$ means "approximately equal to" for example, $13 \div 3 \approx 4$.

Estimating fractions

You can estimate fractions and proportions by comparing quantities with fractions you can picture in your head. For example:

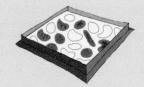

Roughly $\frac{3}{4}$ of this cake is left, so about $\frac{1}{4}$ of it has been eaten.

There are about as many spaces as chocolates: almost half the chocolates are left.

Estimating using rounding

You can estimate the answer to a problem by rounding the numbers to ones that are easier to deal with. That way, when you've done your final calculation, you'll know if you've got a sensible answer.

Calculation methods

There are three main ways to work out the exact answer to a math puzzle. You could do the calculation in your head (this is called a mental calculation) or write out a full calculation on paper. For speed, you might use a calculator or even a computer.

Find out more about: dividing (pages 46-61); **multiplying** (pages 46-59); **proportions** (page 29); **rounding** (page 33); **using calculators** (pages 64-66)

Adding and subtracting

Adding finds the total of two or more numbers or quantities, or increases something by some amount. Subtracting takes one number or quantity away from another, or reduces something by some amount. Adding and subtracting are the opposite, or inverse, of each other.

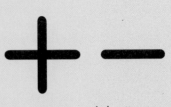

The plus sign (+) tells you to add. The minus sign (−) tells you to subtract.

Aspects of adding

There are two ways of thinking about adding. One aspect of adding is putting two quantities together, and finding out how much there is altogether. This tells you what the total of the two quantities is. For example, you have a bag of 5 marbles and your friend has a bag of 8 marbles. If you pour all the marbles into one big bag then count them, you find out how many there are altogether.

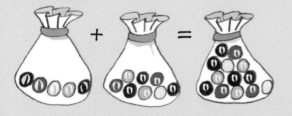

You can write this as:

$$5 + 8 = 13$$

The total when you add together two or more numbers is called the sum. For example, the sum of 5 and 8 is 13.

"Putting together" words include:

altogether	total
sum	plus

The other aspect of adding is increasing a quantity by some amount, and finding out what you've increased the original quantity to. For example, if you have 5 marbles in a bag and you put three more marbles into the same bag, you find out the new number of marbles by counting on from the original amount.

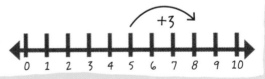

You can show this on a number line:

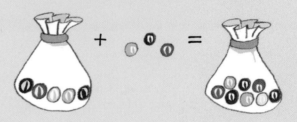

You can write this as:

$$5 + 3 = 8$$

"Increasing" words include:

increase by	count on	plus
more	go up by	

Aspects of subtracting

One aspect of subtracting is removing some objects from a quantity. For example, you have a bag of 8 marbles and 3 drop out. If you count the marbles in the bag, you are finding out how many are left.

You can write this as:

$$8 - 3 = 5$$

"Removing" words include:

take away	reduce	subtract
remove	left	

Another aspect of subtracting is separating a quantity into two quantities. This is called partitioning. For example, you have 15 marbles and you put 6 in one bag and 9 in another bag. You haven't removed any marbles but you have separated them.

You can write this as:

$$15 = 6 + 9$$
$$or \quad 15 - 9 = 6$$
$$or \quad 15 - 6 = 9$$

"Partitioning" questions include:

how many in this group?
how many in that group?
how many altogether?

Yet another aspect of subtracting is to reduce a quantity by some amount. This is counting back. For example, if the price of the bag of marbles is reduced by 3 cents from 18 cents, you can count back from 18 cents to find the new price (15 cents).

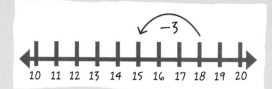

You can write this as:

$$18 - 3 = 15$$

"Reducing" words include:

count back	decrease by	less than
go down by	go back by	subtract

A further aspect of subtracting is comparison, which means you compare quantities without removing any. For example, if you have a bag of 12 marbles and a bag of 16 marbles, you can compare them in these ways:

What is the difference between the number of marbles in the first bag and the number of marbles in the second bag?

How many more marbles are in the second bag than the first?

How many fewer marbles are in the first bag than the second bag?

You can write these out as:

$$16 - 12 = 4$$

Comparison is the form of subtraction that people use most often in everyday life.

> "Comparing" questions include:
>
> what is the difference?
> how many more?
> how many fewer?
> how much greater?
> how much less?
> how much smaller?

Addition and subtraction facts

Although you can always work out every calculation from scratch, you will find it much quicker and easier if you learn the following number facts:

Addition pairs up to 20

Once you know the addition pairs on this grid, you can work out subtraction facts, too. For example, $3 + 4 = 7$ so $7 - 4 = 3$.

+	0	1	2	3	4	5	6	7	8	9	10
0	0	1	2	3	4	5	6	7	8	9	10
1	1	2	3	4	5	6	7	8	9	10	11
2	2	3	4	5	6	7	8	9	10	11	12
3	3	4	5	6	7	8	9	10	11	12	13
4	4	5	6	7	8	9	10	11	12	13	14
5	5	6	7	8	9	10	11	12	13	14	15
6	6	7	8	9	10	11	12	13	14	15	16
7	7	8	9	10	11	12	13	14	15	16	17
8	8	9	10	11	12	13	14	15	16	17	18
9	9	10	11	12	13	14	15	16	17	18	19
10	10	11	12	13	14	15	16	17	18	19	20

Addition pairs that make 10

0	10
1	9
2	8
3	7
4	6
5	5
6	4
7	3
8	2
9	1
10	0

The pairs of numbers in each row add up to 10. For example:

$0 + 10 = 10$

$1 + 9 = 10$

and so on.

Subtraction is the opposite of addition, so if you know the pairs of numbers that add up to 10, you also know, for example, that:

$10 - 0 = 10$

$10 - 1 = 9$

and so on,

and also that

$10 - 10 = 0$

$10 - 9 = 1$

and so on.

Addition pairs that make 100

These pairs of numbers all add up to 100. For example:

$0 + 100 = 100$

$10 + 90 = 100$

and so on.

Subtraction is the opposite of addition, so if you know the pairs of numbers that add up to 100, you also know, for example, that:

$100 - 0 = 100$

$100 - 10 = 90$

and so on,

and also that

$100 - 100 = 0$

$100 - 90 = 10$

and so on.

0	100
10	90
20	80
30	70
40	60
50	50
60	40
70	30
80	20
90	10
100	0

Laws of addition

There are two useful things to learn about the way adding works. You can write these laws using algebra, where letters stand for numbers. This way you can see the rules work for any numbers, as long as value a is the same as a, b is the same as b, and c is the same as c.

Order

It doesn't matter what order you add numbers in: the answer is always the same. This is called the commutative law of addition and you write it as: $a + b = b + a$. For example:

$$5 + 3 = 3 + 5 = 8$$

Grouping

Parentheses ( ) around numbers tell you which part of a calculation to work out first. But if the calculation only contains adding, the grouping doesn't affect the answer. This is called the associative law of addition, written as: $(a + b) + c = a + (b + c)$.
For example:

$$(2 + 6) + 3 = 2 + (6 + 3) = 11$$

Adding and subtracting positive and negative numbers

Subtracting a negative number gives the same answer as adding a positive number. Adding a negative number gives the same answer as subtracting a positive number. This means that if two symbols next to each other in a calculation are the same, you add. If they are different, subtract. (Remember: a number without a symbol is positive.) For example:

$$4 + 3 = 7 \qquad 4 + (-3) = 1$$
$$4 - (-3) = 7 \qquad 4 - 3 = 1$$

Mental addition

There are several ways to add numbers in your head, so you need to look at the numbers and decide which method will work best. When you do mental calculations, you may need to jot down some numbers as you go.

Adding by splitting up numbers

Some calculations are easier if you break up one or more of the numbers into smaller numbers, and add them in stages. This is called partitioning. For example:

$$72 + 16$$
$$= 72 + 10 + 6$$
$$= 82 + 6$$
$$= 88$$

$$147 + 64$$
$$= 140 + 7 + 60 + 4$$
$$= 140 + 60 + 7 + 4$$
$$= 200 + 11$$
$$= 211$$

Adding using place value

You can use what you know about place value to add numbers together. For example, 200 and 500 are one hundred times bigger than 2 and 5, so if:

$$2 + 5 = 7$$
$$\text{then } 200 + 500 = 700$$
$$\text{and } 2,000 + 5,000 = 7,000$$

This works for decimals too. For example:

$$0.2 + 0.5 = 0.7$$
$$\text{and } 0.02 + 0.05 = 0.07$$

Adding by rounding and compensating

A quick way to add numbers together is to round one of them to the nearest ten and add this number instead. You will then need to change your answer a little, by adding or subtracting to make up for the rounding. This is called compensating.

If you rounded up, your answer will be too high, so you compensate by taking away the rounding amount. For example:

$$36 + 48$$

Round 48 up to 50 by adding 2. Then do the calculation with 50 instead:

$$36 + 50 = 86$$

Subtract the 2 you rounded up by:

$$86 - 2 = 84$$

so

$$36 + 48 = 84$$

If you rounded down, your answer will be too low, so compensate by adding the rounding amount. For example:

$$38 + 61$$

Round 61 down to 60 by subtracting 1. Then do the calculation with 60:

$$38 + 60 = 98$$

Add the 1 you rounded down by:

$$98 + 1 = 99$$

so

$$38 + 61 = 99$$

Compensating rules

You can add any numbers by rounding and compensating, but it works particularly well with numbers that end in 1, 2, 8 or 9.

Number ends in:	Round...	Compensate by:
1, 2, 3, 4	Down	+ 1, 2, 3, 4
5, 6, 7, 8, 9	Up	− 5, 6, 7, 8, 9

Adding using near doubles

If two numbers are almost equal, double the smaller number and add the difference between them. Or, you can double the larger number and subtract the difference. For example:

$$123 + 126$$

These numbers are almost equal (the difference is 3) so you can use either:

$$123 \times 2 = 246$$
$$246 + 3 = 249$$

or

$$126 \times 2 = 252$$
$$252 - 3 = 249$$

Adding by spotting pairs

If you need to add a list of numbers in your head, look for pairs of numbers that add up to 10 or 100. For example:

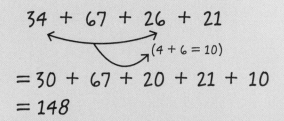

$$34 + 67 + 26 + 21$$
$$(4 + 6 = 10)$$

$$= 30 + 67 + 20 + 21 + 10$$
$$= 148$$

Find out more about: adding (pages 35-42); addition pairs to 10 and 100 (page 37); doubling (page 46); rounding (page 33); subtracting (pages 35-45)

Adding with a number line

First imagine an empty number line that starts with the larger number in the calculation. Then imagine jumping along the line as you add each place value of the other number, to give your answer.

Partition the number you are adding into tens and ones. Add its tens first, then its ones. For example: **35 + 54** *(35 = 30 + 5)*

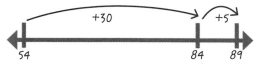

Or:

Partition the number you are adding into tens and ones. Add its tens. Partition the ones again, so you can "step up" to the next ten. Add the remaining ones. For example: **27 + 28** *(27 = 20 + 2 + 5)*

Or:

You can sometimes partition the ones first to "bounce off" the next ten. For example: **38 + 47** *(38 = 3 + 5 + 30)*

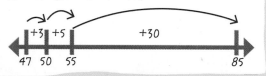

Adding hundreds, tens and ones

You can add numbers by adding each place value in turn, starting with the highest. Next, add the totals. For example:

54 + 22

$50 + 20 = 70$	*Add the tens.*
$4 + 2 = 6$	*Add the ones.*
$70 + 6 = 76$	*Add the totals.*

123 + 168

$100 + 100 = 200$	*Add the hundreds.*
$20 + 60 = 80$	*Add the tens.*
$3 + 8 = 11$	*Add the ones.*
$200 + 80 + 11 = 291$	*Add the totals.*

You could also do a calculation that needs you to make an adjustment in one or more of the place value "columns" and still keep it all in your head. For example:

153 + 168

$100 + 100 = 200$	*Add the hundreds.*
$50 + 60 = 110$	*Add the tens.*
$3 + 8 = 11$	*Add the ones.*
$200 + 110 + 11 = 321$	*Add the totals.*

Adding using a number grid

You can use this number grid to help you add two numbers. Find one number on the grid. Then move down a square for each ten you want to add, and along one square to the right for each one you want to add. For example, for 45 + 34, find 45, move down 3 squares (this adds 30) and along 4 squares (to add 4). The answer is 79.

This number grid shows the numbers from 1 to 100.

1	2	3	4	5	6	7	8	9	10
11	12	13	14	15	16	(17)	18	19	20
21	22	23	24	25	26	27	28	29	30
31	32	33	34	35	36	37	38	39	40
41	42	43	44	45	46	47	48	49	50
51	52	53	54	55	56	57	58	(59)	60
61	62	63	64	65	66	67	68	69	70
71	72	73	74	75	76	77	78	79	80
81	82	83	84	85	86	87	88	89	90
91	92	93	94	95	96	97	98	99	100

To use a number grid to subtract numbers, move up a square for each ten you want to subtract, then along one square to the left for each one you want to subtract. For example, for 59 – 42, find 59, move up 4 squares (to subtract 40) and back 2 squares (to subtract 2). The answer is 17.

Written addition

If you can't do a calculation in your head, you may need to work it out on paper. The most common way is the column method. It works for numbers of any size, including decimals. Write the calculation out as shown below, lining up the ones, tens and so on. Starting with the lowest place value (on the right), add the digits in each column and write the answer between the lines.

Step 1

$$\begin{array}{r} 6\ 5 \\ +\ 3\ 2 \\ \hline \\ \hline \end{array}$$

To add 65 and 32, first write them down one above the other with the ones and tens lined up.

Step 2

$$\begin{array}{r} 6\ 5 \\ +\ 3\ 2 \\ \hline 7 \end{array}$$

The ones column has the lowest place value, so add it first.

Step 3

$$\begin{array}{r} 6\ 5 \\ +\ 3\ 2 \\ \hline 9\ 7 \\ \hline \end{array}$$

Add the tens column next.

This is the answer: 65 + 32 = 97.

This example shows the method, but you would usually add 2-digit numbers in your head.

If the digits in a column add up to 10 or more, write the ones between lines, and write down the tens under the next column. This is often called carrying over. Then add the number you have carried over to the total of the next column. For example:

Step 1

$$\begin{array}{r} 4\ 5 \\ +\ 6\ 7 \\ \hline \\ \hline \end{array}$$

To add 45 and 67, first write them down one above the other with the ones and tens lined up.

Step 2

$$\begin{array}{r} 4\ 5 \\ +\ 6\ 7 \\ \hline 2 \\ \hline {\scriptstyle 1} \end{array}$$

The ones column has the lowest place value, so add it first. 5 + 7 = 12, so write down the ones (2), and carry the tens (1) to add to the next column.

Step 3

$$\begin{array}{r} 4\ 5 \\ +\ 6\ 7 \\ \hline 1\ 2 \\ \hline {\scriptstyle 1}\ \ {\scriptstyle 1} \end{array}$$

4 + 6 + 1 = 11. Write down the ones (1), and carry the tens (1) to add to the next column.

Step 4

$$\begin{array}{r} 4\ 5 \\ +\ 6\ 7 \\ \hline 1\ 1\ 2 \\ \hline {\scriptstyle 1}\ \ {\scriptstyle 1} \end{array}$$

There are no more hundreds to add, so write the 1 between the lines to finish the answer: 45 + 67 = 112

This example shows the method, but you would usually add 2-digit numbers in your head.

The column method works for numbers of any size. For example:

3-digit numbers

$$\begin{array}{r} 1\ 7\ 4 \\ +\ \ \ 2\ 1 \\ \hline 1\ 9\ 5 \\ \hline \end{array}$$

4-digit numbers

$$\begin{array}{r} 2{,}5\ 1\ 3 \\ +\ 1{,}4\ 6\ 5 \\ \hline 3{,}9\ 7\ 8 \\ \hline \end{array}$$

You can carry over to the hundreds and thousands columns too. For example:

3-digit numbers

$$\begin{array}{r} 2\ 4\ 8 \\ +6\ 7\ 3 \\ \hline 9\ 2\ 1 \\ \hline {\scriptstyle 1}\ \ {\scriptstyle 1} \end{array}$$

4-digit numbers

$$\begin{array}{r} 7{,}4\ 9\ 5 \\ +\ 4{,}6\ 0\ 8 \\ \hline 1\ 2{,}1\ 0\ 3 \\ \hline {\scriptstyle 1}\ \ {\scriptstyle 1}\ \ {\scriptstyle 1} \end{array}$$

Find out more about: decimals (pages 21-24)

Checking additions

There are different ways to check your adding.

Approximating

You can use rounding to see if your answer is sensible. For example, if you calculated that $143 + 39 = 182$, you can check your answer by:

Rounding up 39 to 40:

$143 + 40 = 183$

Rounding up makes the answer too big: the correct answer is less than 183.

Rounding down 143 to 140:

$140 + 39 = 179$

Rounding down makes the answer too small: the correct answer is more than 179.

You can use number facts to work out the last digit. For example:

$3 + 9 = 12$

So your answer to $143 + 39$ should end in a 2.

For a more accurate check, you can round and compensate. For example:

$143 + 40 = 183 - 1$

Rearranging the calculation

You can rearrange the calculation and check your answer by adding in a different order, or by subtracting. For example, if $143 + 39 = 182$:

$39 + 143 = 182$
$182 - 143 = 39$
$182 - 39 = 143$

To remind you which numbers to add or subtract, you could use a pair of numbers whose addition pairs you know. For example:

$5 + 3 = 8$	$a + b = c$
$8 - 5 = 3$	$c - a = b$
$8 - 3 = 5$	$c - b = a$

Mental subtraction

You can subtract any numbers using written methods, but there are several ways to subtract numbers in your head too. Before you start, look at the numbers and decide which method to use. For example, you could use written methods to work out $7{,}003 - 6{,}988$, but all you need to do is count up from the lower number, and you can do this in your head:

$6{,}988 + 2$ *is* $6{,}990$
then $+ 10$ *is* $7{,}000$
then $+ 3$ *is* $7{,}003$

The difference is $2 + 10 + 3$, which is 15.

or $6{,}988 + 10$ *is* $6{,}998$
then $+ 2$ *is* $7{,}000$
then $+ 3$ *is* $7{,}003$

The difference is $10 + 2 + 3$, which is 15.

Subtracting by counting on

You can use addition to subtract, by counting on from the lower number to the higher number to find the difference between them.

You might find it helpful to imagine an empty number line that starts with the number you want to take away. Imagine jumping along to the next multiple of 10, and then jumping again to the number that you are taking away from. Then add up these jumps to find the answer.

For example, to subtract 37 from 82:

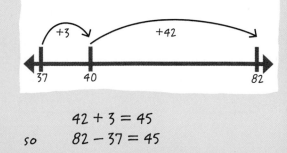

$42 + 3 = 45$

so $82 - 37 = 45$

Find out more about: addition pairs (page 37); **digits** (page 7); **multiples** (page 9); **number lines** (page 8); **rounding** (page 33); **rounding and compensating in addition** (page 38)

Subtracting friendly numbers

Sometimes you can make a subtraction easier by using "more friendly" numbers. You can do this by breaking up the number you are taking away into smaller numbers, and subtracting them in stages. (This is called partitioning.) For example:

$$832 - 437$$

This is much easier if you turn it into:

$$832 - 432 - 5$$

This gives you 400 – 5, which is easy:

$$400 - 5 = 395$$

$$1,296 - 597$$

This is much easier if you turn it into:

$$1,296 - 596 - 1$$

This gives you 700 – 1, which is easy:

$$700 - 1 = 699$$

It's important always to subtract numbers in the order they are given, otherwise your answer may be wrong. For example:

$$832 - 432 - 5 = 395 \quad ✓$$
$$\text{but} \quad 432 - 5 - 832 = -405 \quad ✗$$

Subtracting using place value

You can use what you know about place value to subtract whole numbers and decimals. For example, 700 and 400 are 100 times bigger than 7 and 4, so if:

$$7 - 4 = 3$$

then you can also calculate that:

$$700 - 400 = 300$$
$$7,000 - 4,000 = 3,000$$
$$0.7 - 0.4 = 0.3$$
$$0.07 - 0.04 = 0.03$$

Subtracting by rounding and compensating

A quick way to subtract numbers is to round one of them to the nearest multiple of 10 and use this number instead. You will then need to compensate, which means adding or subtracting to make up for the rounding. To work out how much you need to compensate by, and whether you need to add or subtract, look at the rounding you've done.

If you round up, your answer will be too high, so you compensate by subtracting the rounding amount. For example:

$$79 - 26$$

Round 79 up to 80 by adding 1. Then do the calculation with 80 instead:

$$80 - 26 = 54$$

Subtract the 1 you rounded up by:

$$54 - 1 = 53$$

so
$$79 - 26 = 53$$

If you rounded down, your answer will be too low. In this case you must compensate by adding the rounding amount. For example:

$$91 - 47$$

Round 91 down to 90 by subtracting 1. Then do the calculation with 90.

$$90 - 47 = 43$$

Add the 1 you rounded down by:

$$43 + 1 = 44$$

so
$$91 - 47 = 44$$

Compensating rules

You can subtract any numbers by rounding and compensating, but it works particularly well with numbers that end in 1, 2, 8 or 9.

Number ends in:	Round...	Compensate by:
1, 2, 3, 4	Down	+ 1, 2, 3, 4
5, 6, 7, 8, 9	Up	− 5, 6, 7, 8, 9

Subtracting hundreds, tens and ones

You can subtract a number by taking away the digit at each place value in turn, starting at the highest place value. Add the differences together to give the total difference. This method works best when digits at each place value in the number you are taking away are smaller than those in the other number. For example:

$54 - 23$ 3 ones are less than 4 ones. 2 tens are less than 5 tens.

$5(0) - 2(0) = 3(0)$ Subtract the tens.

$4 - 3 = 1$ Subtract the ones.

$30 + 1 = 31$ Add the results.

$169 - 43$ 3 ones are less than 9 ones. 4 tens are less than 6 tens.

$1(00) - 0 = 1(00)$ Subtract the hundreds.

$6(0) - 4(0) = 2(0)$ Subtract the tens.

$9 - 3 = 6$ Subtract the ones.

$100 + 20 + 6 = 126$ Add the results.

Written subtraction

The most common way of subtracting on paper is called the column method. It works for numbers of any size, including decimals. Write the calculation out with the larger number above the smaller one, lining up the ones, tens and so on. Start at the right with the lowest place value column, and subtract the bottom digits from the top ones. For example:

Step 1

$$\begin{array}{r} 7\ 6 \\ -\ 2\ 4 \\ \hline \end{array}$$

To subtract 24 from 76, first write the numbers down one above the other with the ones and tens lined up.

Step 2

$$\begin{array}{r} 7\ 6 \\ -\ 2\ 4 \\ \hline 2 \end{array}$$

The ones column has the lowest place value, so start your subtraction here. Take the bottom number from the top one.

Step 3

$$\begin{array}{r} 7\ 6 \\ -\ 2\ 4 \\ \hline 5\ 2 \end{array}$$

Subtract in the tens column next.

This is the answer: $76 - 24 = 52$.

This example shows the method, but you would usually subtract 2-digit numbers in your head.

The method works for numbers of any size. For example:

3-digit numbers
$$\begin{array}{r} 2\ 8\ 9 \\ -\ 1\ 4\ 1 \\ \hline 1\ 4\ 8 \end{array}$$

4-digit numbers
$$\begin{array}{r} 6,9\ 5\ 5 \\ -\ 4,1\ 4\ 3 \\ \hline 2,8\ 1\ 2 \end{array}$$

Find out more about: **decimals** (pages 21–24); **difference** (page 37); **digits** (page 7); **place value** (page 8); **rounding and compensating in subtraction** (page 43)

Column method continued

If the top digit is less than the bottom one, you can use a value from the next column on the left. This is called exchanging. You then need to adjust that column before you finish your calculation. For example:

Step 1

$$8\ 3$$
$$-\ 6\ 9$$

To subtract 69 from 83, first write the numbers down one above the other with the ones and tens lined up.

Step 2

$$^7\cancel{8}\ ^1 3$$
$$-\ 6\ 9$$

The ones column has the lowest place value, so start subtracting here. 3 is less than 9, so exchange one of the tens for ten ones, and add these to the 3, to make 13. Remember to change the 8(0) to 7(0).

Step 3

$$^7\cancel{8}\ ^1 3$$
$$-\ 6\ 9$$
$$4$$

Next subtract the ones column: $13 - 9 = 4$.

Step 4

$$^7\cancel{8}\ ^1 3$$
$$-\ 6\ 9$$
$$1\ 4$$

Finish the calculation by subtracting the tens column: $7(0) - 6(0) = 1(0)$

This is the answer: $83 - 69 = 14$.

This example shows the method, but you would usually subtract 2-digit numbers in your head.

The method works for numbers of any size. For example:

3-digit numbers

$$^5\cancel{6}\ ^{13}\cancel{4}\ ^1 2$$
$$-\ 4\ 7\ 4$$
$$1\ 6\ 8$$

4-digit numbers

$$^4\cancel{5},\ ^{11}\cancel{2}\ ^9\cancel{0}\ ^1 5$$
$$-\ 2,\ 7\ 2\ 6$$
$$2,\ 4\ 7\ 9$$

Checking subtractions

There are different ways to check your subtracting.

Approximating

You can use rounding to see if your answer is sensible. For example, if you calculated that $179 - 53 = 126$, you can check your answer by:

Rounding up 179 to 180:

$$180 - 53 = 127$$

Rounding up the number you are taking away from makes the answer too big: the correct answer is less than 127.

Rounding down 53 to 50:

$$179 - 50 = 129$$

Rounding down the number you are taking away makes the answer too big too: the correct answer is less than 129.

You can use number facts to work out the last digit. For example:

$$9 - 3 = 6$$

So your answer to $179 - 53$ should end in a 6.

Rearranging the calculation

You can rearrange the calculation and check your answer by subtracting in a different order, or by adding.

For example, if $134 - 53 = 81$:

$$134 - 81 = 53$$
$$81 + 53 = 134$$
$$53 + 81 = 134$$

To remind you which numbers to add or subtract, you could use a pair of numbers whose addition pairs you know. For example:

$5 + 3 = 8$	$a + b = c$
$8 - 5 = 3$	$c - a = b$
$8 - 3 = 5$	$c - b = a$

Find out more about: addition pairs (page 37); digits (page 7); place value (page 8); rounding (page 33)

Multiplying and dividing

Multiplying is a quick way of adding together several sets of the same number or quantity. Dividing is a quick way of subtracting several sets of the same number or quantity, or splitting it up into equal groups. Multiplying and dividing are the opposite, or inverse, of each other.

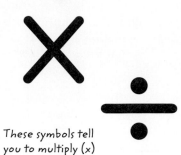

These symbols tell you to multiply (x) and divide (÷).

Aspects of multiplying

Multiplying has different meanings. One aspect of multiplying is repeated adding. For example, if you have 3 bags with 10 marbles in each bag and want to find out how many marbles you have altogether, you can multiply 10 by 3. You can write this as:

$$10 \times 3 = 30$$

   x 3

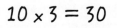
is the same as

Repeated adding is the inverse (opposite) of repeated subtracting.

"Repeated adding" words include:

so many sets of   sets of
how many sets of?   groups of
how many altogether?

The other main aspect of multiplying is scaling. For example, if you have 4 giant marbles, and you trade each one for 5 of your friend's small marbles, you'll end up with 20 small marbles. You can write this as:

$$4 \times 5 = 20$$

is scaled up to

"Scaling" words include:

multiplied by   times as large
for every   times as big
for each   times as much
double (x2)   triple (x3)

Products

The result when you multiply numbers is the product. For example, when you multiply 3 by 10, the product is 30.

Aspects of dividing

Dividing has different meanings. One aspect of dividing is sharing. For example, if you share a bag of 30 marbles between yourself and two friends, dividing will tell you how many marbles each person gets.

"Sharing" words include:

sharing equally between
how many each?

Another aspect of dividing is grouping. For example, you have 30 marbles and want to give 3 to each of your friends. Dividing will tell you how many friends you can give marbles to. This is repeated subtracting, which is the inverse (opposite) of repeated adding.

"Grouping" questions include:

how many sets / sets of?
how many groups / groups of?

You can show dividing in several ways. For example, you can write 30 divided by 3 as:

$$30 \div 3 \qquad \frac{30}{3} \qquad 30/3 \qquad 3\overline{)30}$$

Quotients and remainders

A quotient is the whole number of times you can divide one number by another. If you can't divide a number exactly, you have an amount left over. This is called the remainder. You can show remainders as whole numbers (with rem. or r. written in front of them), or write them as fractions or decimals. For example, $10 \div 4 = 2$ rem. 2, or 2 r.2, or $2\frac{1}{2}$ or 2.5.

Divisors

The divisor is the number you divide by. For example, in $6 \div 3$ the divisor is 3.

Rounding after dividing

Sometimes you may need to round an answer up or down. Which way you round your answer will depend on what you divided and why. For example:

A van takes 8 children. How many vans do you need to take 30 children to a wildlife park?

$$30 \div 8 = 3 \, r. \, 6$$
Round up to 4.

Here you must round up, or you'll leave some children behind, so you need four vans.

A driver fills up his truck with 30 gallons of gas. He uses 8 gallons of gas on each delivery trip. How many delivery trips can he sensibly make before filling the tank again?

$$30 \div 8 = 3 \, r. \, 6$$
Round down to 3.

Here you must round down, or the truck will run out of gas on the way, so the man can only make three trips.

Opposite effects

Multiplying and dividing are the inverse, or opposite, of each other. This means you can "undo" one operation by using the other one. For example:

$$2 \times 3 = 6$$
and $$6 \div 3 = 2$$

Find out more about: decimals (pages 21-24); **fractions** (pages 16-20); **rounding** (page 33)

Times tables

Times tables are lists of multiplication facts. As well as helping you multiply in an instant, knowing times tables will help you work out other number facts, too. For example, if you know that $3 \times 2 = 6$, here are some related facts you can find:

$2 \times 3 = 6$ — because you can multiply numbers in any order.

$6 \div 2 = 3$
$6 \div 3 = 2$ — because division "undoes" multiplication.

$0.2 \times 0.3 = 0.06$
$600 \div 300 = 2$ — because the digits are 2, 3 and 6, but they have different place values.

Some times tables are closely related to each other, so you can often use one to work out another. For example:

Double the 2 times table (add it to itself) to get the 4 times table.

Double the 2 times table twice to get the 8 times table.

Double the 3 times table to get the 6 times table... and so on.

You can work out the 9 times table from the 10 times table, like this:

$9 \times 1 = (1 \times 10) - 1 = 9$
$9 \times 2 = (2 \times 10) - 2 = 18$
$9 \times 3 = (3 \times 10) - 3 = 27$

... and so on.

Double tricks

To multiply a number by 4, double it then double the result. To multiply by 8, double, double and double again. For example:

$16 \times 4 = 16 \times 2 \times 2$
$= 32 \times 2 = 64$

5x table trick

You can use this handy method to multiply anything by 5:

Divide even numbers by 2 and write 0 after the result. For example:

$16 \times 5 = 80$ $48 \times 5 = 240$
$(16 \div 2 = 8)$ $(48 \div 2 = 24)$

Subtract 1 from odd numbers, then divide by 2 and write 5 after the result. For example:

$19 \times 5 = 95$ $51 \times 5 = 255$
$(19 - 1 = 18$ $(51 - 1 = 50$
$18 \div 2 = 9)$ $50 \div 2 = 25)$

9x table trick

You can use your fingers to help you remember the 9x table up to 10×9. For example, to work out 4×9, hold your hands up with your palms facing you, then fold down your 4th finger from the left. The number of fingers on the left of the folded finger shows the tens digit, and the number of fingers on the right of it give you the ones digit.

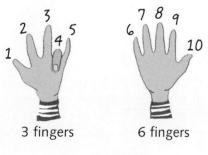

3 fingers   6 fingers

$4 \times 9 = 36$

To work out 5×9, hold down the 5th finger, and so on.

11x table tricks

To multiply numbers from 1 to 9 by 11, write the number twice. For example:

$$11 \times 2 = 22 \text{ and } 11 \times 7 = 77$$

To multiply a 2-digit number by 11, write its digits with a space in between. Then add the digits and write their sum in the space:

$$26 \times 11 = 2 \ ? \ 6 = 286$$
$$2 + 6 = 8$$

If their sum is more than 9, "carry" the 1 and add it to the first digit. For example:

$$82 \times 11 = 8 \ ? \ 2 = 902$$
$$8 + 2 = 10$$
$$8 + 1 = 9$$

3 x table

3	×	1	=	3
3	×	2	=	6
3	×	3	=	9
3	×	4	=	12
3	×	5	=	15
3	×	6	=	18
3	×	7	=	21
3	×	8	=	24
3	×	9	=	27
3	×	10	=	30
3	×	11	=	33
3	×	12	=	36

2 x table

2	×	1	=	2
2	×	2	=	4
2	×	3	=	6
2	×	4	=	8
2	×	5	=	10
2	×	6	=	12
2	×	7	=	14
2	×	8	=	16
2	×	9	=	18
2	×	10	=	20
2	×	11	=	22
2	×	12	=	24

4 x table

4	×	1	=	4
4	×	2	=	8
4	×	3	=	12
4	×	4	=	16
4	×	5	=	20
4	×	6	=	24
4	×	7	=	28
4	×	8	=	32
4	×	9	=	36
4	×	10	=	40
4	×	11	=	44
4	×	12	=	48

Find out more about: digits (page 7); **sum** (page 35)

5 x table

5	x	1	=	5
5	x	2	=	10
5	x	3	=	15
5	x	4	=	20
5	x	5	=	25
5	x	6	=	30
5	x	7	=	35
5	x	8	=	40
5	x	9	=	45
5	x	10	=	50
5	x	11	=	55
5	x	12	=	60

7 x table

7	x	1	=	7
7	x	2	=	14
7	x	3	=	21
7	x	4	=	28
7	x	5	=	35
7	x	6	=	42
7	x	7	=	49
7	x	8	=	56
7	x	9	=	63
7	x	10	=	70
7	x	11	=	77
7	x	12	=	84

6 x table

6	x	1	=	6
6	x	2	=	12
6	x	3	=	18
6	x	4	=	24
6	x	5	=	30
6	x	6	=	36
6	x	7	=	42
6	x	8	=	48
6	x	9	=	54
6	x	10	=	60
6	x	11	=	66
6	x	12	=	72

8 x table

8	x	1	=	8
8	x	2	=	16
8	x	3	=	24
8	x	4	=	32
8	x	5	=	40
8	x	6	=	48
8	x	7	=	56
8	x	8	=	64
8	x	9	=	72
8	x	10	=	80
8	x	11	=	88
8	x	12	=	96

9 x table

9	x	1	=	9
9	x	2	=	18
9	x	3	=	27
9	x	4	=	36
9	x	5	=	45
9	x	6	=	54
9	x	7	=	63
9	x	8	=	72
9	x	9	=	81
9	x	10	=	90
9	x	11	=	99
9	x	12	=	108

11 x table

11	x	1	=	11
11	x	2	=	22
11	x	3	=	33
11	x	4	=	44
11	x	5	=	55
11	x	6	=	66
11	x	7	=	77
11	x	8	=	88
11	x	9	=	99
11	x	10	=	110
11	x	11	=	121
11	x	12	=	132

10 x table

10	x	1	=	10
10	x	2	=	20
10	x	3	=	30
10	x	4	=	40
10	x	5	=	50
10	x	6	=	60
10	x	7	=	70
10	x	8	=	80
10	x	9	=	90
10	x	10	=	100
10	x	11	=	110
10	x	12	=	120

12 x table

12	x	1	=	12
12	x	2	=	24
12	x	3	=	36
12	x	4	=	48
12	x	5	=	60
12	x	6	=	72
12	x	7	=	84
12	x	8	=	96
12	x	9	=	108
12	x	10	=	120
12	x	11	=	132
12	x	12	=	144

Multiplying using a grid

You can use a multiplication grid like the one below, to help you find the product of two numbers. For example:

To work out 4 x 7, find 4 on the first row and 7 in the first column. Then follow the grid in a straight line down from the 4 and across from the 7. The square where the paths cross contains the answer (28).

×	1	2	3	4	5	6	7	8	9	10
1	1	2	3	4	5	6	7	8	9	10
2	2	4	6	8	10	12	14	16	18	20
3	3	6	9	12	15	18	21	24	27	30
4	4	8	12	16	20	24	28	32	36	40
5	5	10	15	20	25	30	35	40	45	50
6	6	12	18	24	30	36	42	48	54	60
7	7	14	21	28	35	42	49	56	63	70
8	8	16	24	32	40	48	56	64	72	80
9	9	18	27	36	45	54	63	72	81	90
10	10	20	30	40	50	60	70	80	90	100

Multiplying by 10

To multiply a number by 10, move all its digits one place to the left. If the number you are multiplying is a whole number, you'll need to write in a zero at the end to fill in the space. For example:

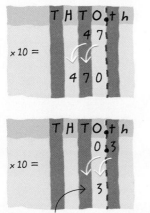

0 in front of a whole number isn't needed, so you can leave it off.

Multiplying by 100 and 1,000

To multiply a number by 100, move all its digits two places to the left. Move the digits three places to the left to multiply by 1,000. If the number you are multiplying is or becomes a whole number, you'll usually need to write in zeros at the end to fill in the spaces. For example:

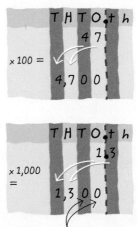

Write in 0s to hold the tens and ones places.

Multiplying by multiples of 10

To multiply by multiples of 10 (such as 20, 300 or 4,000) multiply the number by the first digit (in this case 2, 3 or 4). Then move the digits of your answer to the left (one, two or three places) and write in zeros on the end if needed. For example:

32×20

$= 32 \times 2 \times 10$

$= 64 \times 10$

$= 640$

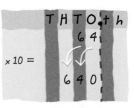

0.5×400

$= 0.5 \times 4 \times 100$

$= 2 \times 100$

$= 200$

Find out more about: multiples (page 9); **place value** (page 8); **products** (page 46); **zero** (page 7)

Dividing using a grid

You can use a multiplication grid like the one below, to help you divide numbers up to 100. For example:

To work out 28 ÷ 4, find 4 on the first row and follow the grid in a straight line down until you come to 28. Then follow the grid across to the first column to find the answer (7).

×	1	2	3	4	5	6	7	8	9	10
1	1	2	3	4	5	6	7	8	9	10
2	2	4	6	8	10	12	14	16	18	20
3	3	6	9	12	15	18	21	24	27	30
4	4	8	12	16	20	24	28	32	36	40
5	5	10	15	20	25	30	35	40	45	50
6	6	12	18	24	30	36	42	48	54	60
7	7	14	21	28	35	42	49	56	63	70
8	8	16	24	32	40	48	56	64	72	80
9	9	18	27	36	45	54	63	72	81	90
10	10	20	30	40	50	60	70	80	90	100

Dividing by 10

To divide a number by 10, move all its digits one place to the right. For example:

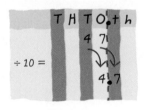

If the original number had a single digit before the decimal point place, write a 0 in front of the decimal point. For example:

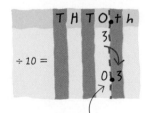

Write in a 0 to hold the ones place.

Dividing by 100 and 1,000

Once you know how to divide by 10, you can use a similar method to divide by 100 and 1,000. To divide a number by 100, move all its digits two places to the right. Move them three places to the right to divide by 1,000. Write in zeros as place holders if you need to. For example:

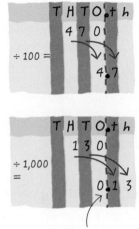

Write in a 0 to hold the ones place.

Dividing by multiples of 10

To divide by multiples of 10 (such as 20, 300 or 4,000) divide the number by the first digit (in this case 2, 3 or 4). Move the digits of your answer to the right (one, two or three places) and write in zeros if needed. For example:

640 ÷ 20
= 640 ÷ 2 ÷ 10
= 320 ÷ 10
= 32

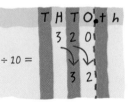

200 ÷ 400
= 200 ÷ 4 ÷ 100
= 50 ÷ 100
= 0.5

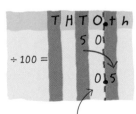

Write in a 0 to hold the ones place.

Find out more about: multiples (page 9); **place value** (page 8); **zero** (page 7)

Laws of multiplication

Here are three useful things to remember about multiplying. You can write these laws using algebra, where letters stand for numbers. This way you can see that they work for any numbers, as long as value a is the same as a, b is the same as b, and c is the same as c.

Trading numbers around

You can multiply numbers in any order: the answer stays the same. This is the commutative law of multiplication and you write it as: $a \times b = b \times a$. For example:

$$5 \times 3 = 3 \times 5 = 15$$

Grouping and regrouping

Parentheses ( ) around numbers show which part of a calculation to do first. But if the calculation only contains multiplication, the grouping doesn't affect the answer. This is called the associative law of multiplication, written as: $(a \times b) \times c = a \times (b \times c)$.

$$(2 \times 6) \times 3 = 2 \times (6 \times 3)$$
$$= 36$$

Breaking it up

Sometimes it's easier to multiply a number if you split it up. This is the distributive law of multiplication: $(a + b) \times c = (a \times c) + (b \times c)$.

$$8 \times 27$$
$$= 8 \times (20 + 7)$$
$$= (8 \times 20) + (8 \times 7)$$
$$= 160 + 56 = 216$$

Divisibility rules

If you can divide a number by another one without leaving a remainder, it is divisible by the number. For example, 8 is divisible by 4 and 2. You can use these tests to see if a number is divisible by another.

Divisible by	Test
2	The last digit is 0, 2, 4, 6, 8.
3	You can divide the sum of the digits by 3.
4	The last two digits make a number you can divide by 4.
5	The last digit is 5 or 0.
6	The last digit is even, and you can divide it by 3.
8	The last three digits make a number you can divide by 8.
9	You can divide the sum of the digits by 9.
10	The last digit is 0.
12	You can divide the number by 3 and 4.
25	The last two digits are 00, 25, 50 or 75.
100	The last two digits are 00.

Multiplying and dividing negative and positive numbers

If you multiply or divide two positive numbers, or two negative numbers, the answer is always positive. If one number is positive and the other is negative, the answer is always negative. For example:

$$2 \times 3 = 6 \qquad 8 \div 4 = 2$$
$$-2 \times -3 = 6 \qquad -8 \div -4 = 2$$
$$-2 \times 3 = -6 \qquad -8 \div 4 = -2$$
$$2 \times -3 = -6 \qquad 8 \div -4 = -2$$

Find out more about: algebra (pages 68-70); **parentheses** (page 62); **negative numbers** (page 7); **positive numbers** (page 7)

Mental multiplication

There are several ways to multiply numbers in your head. Before you start, look at the numbers and decide which method you think will work best.

Multiplying by splitting up numbers

Some calculations are easier to do if you break up one or more of the numbers into smaller numbers, and multiply them in stages. This method is called distribution. For example:

27×3

$= (20 \times 3) + (7 \times 3)$

$= 60 + 21$

$= 81$

Multiplying using repeated addition

Turn a mental multiplication into repeated mental addition. For example:

34×3

$= 34 + 34 + 34$

$= 68 + 34$

$= 102$

Multiplying using place value

You can use what you know about place value to multiply whole numbers and decimals. For example:

If $\quad 2 \times 6 = 12$

then $\quad 200 \times 600 = 120,000$

and $\quad 0.2 \times 0.6 = 0.12$

Multiplying by rounding and compensating

A quick way to multiply numbers is to round one of them to the nearest 10 and use this number instead. You will then need to adjust your answer to make up for the rounding. This is called compensating. (There are some useful hints about compensating on page 56.)

If you rounded up, your answer will be too high, so you must compensate by subtracting. For example:

29×4

Round 29 up to 30 and do the calculation with 30 instead:

$30 \times 4 = 120$

Subtract the amount you rounded up by. This was 1 set of $4 = 4$:

$120 - 4 = 116$

so

$29 \times 4 = 116$

If you rounded down, your answer will be too low, so compensate by adding. For example:

42×6

Round 42 down to 40, then do the calculation with 40.

$40 \times 6 = 240$

Add the amount you rounded down by. This was 2 sets of $6 = 12$:

$240 + 12 = 252$

so

$42 \times 6 = 252$

Find out more about: adding (pages 35-42); **decimals** (pages 21-24); **place value** (page 8); **rounding** (page 33); **whole numbers** (page 7)

Compensating rules

You can multiply any numbers by rounding and compensating, but it works particularly well with numbers that end in 1, 2, 8 or 9.

Number ends in:	Round...	Compensate by:
1, 2, 3, 4	Down	+ 1x, 2x, 3x, 4x
5, 6, 7, 8, 9	Up	− 5x, 6x, 7x, 8x, 9x

(x is the number you multiplied by. So 2x means twice the number you multiplied by, and so on.)

Changing the order of numbers

You can rearrange the numbers in a multiplication calculation, and multiply them in a different order. For example:

Instead of

8×7

try

7×8

$= 56$

Instead of

$10 \times 5 \times 16$

try

$16 \times 5 \times 10$

$= 80 \times 10$

$= 800$

Doubling numbers

Doubling a number is the same as multiplying it by 2 or adding it to itself. To double any 2-digit number in your head, double the tens, double the ones, then add them together. For example:

53×2

$= (50 \times 2) + (3 \times 2)$

$= 100 + 6$

$= 106$

Doubling and halving

Another way you can use numbers that are easier to work with is to double one of the numbers, do the multiplication and halve the answer (divide it by 2). For example:

28×5

Double the 5 and use 10 instead.

$28 \times 10 = 280$

$280 \div 2 = 140$

Halve the answer.

$28 \times 5 = 140$

Multiplying using factors

Sometimes it helps to split up numbers into factors and rearrange the order so they're easier to multiply. For example:

35×16

$= 5 \times 7 \times 4 \times 4$ Break the numbers into factors.

$= (5 \times 4) \times 4 \times 7$

$= (20 \times 4) \times 7$ Rearrange the numbers so they are easier to multiply.

$= 80 \times 7$

$= 560$

Here are some useful factor combinations to try:

To multiply by:	You could:
4	x 2 then x 2
6	x 3 then x 2
8	x 2 three times or x 4 then x 2
9	x 3 then x 3
12	x 4 then x 3
14	x 7 then x 2
15	x 5 then x 3
16	x 4 then x 4

Written multiplication

If you can't do a calculation in your head, here are two ways of multiplying on paper.

Grid method

Break the numbers up into tens and ones and write them along the top and side of a grid like the one below. Multiply each pair of numbers in turn. Then add their totals together. For example:

26 x 45

Step 1
Break each number into tens and ones and write them along the edges of a grid.

×	40	5
20		
6		

Step 2
Multiply each number along the top by each number down the side to complete the grid.

×	40	5
20	800	100
6	240	30

Step 3
Add the products in each row.

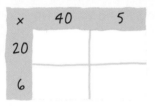

×	40	5	
20	800	100	9 0 0
6	240	30	+ 2 7 0

Step 4
Add together the totals.   1, 1 7 0

so

26 x 45 = 1,170

You can use the grid method to multiply numbers that have 3 or more digits in them, too. Just remember that you need a column for each digit in the largest number, then fill in the grid and add the totals as before. For instance, if the largest number has 3 digits in it, you will need 3 columns in your grid. If it has 4 digits in it, you'll need 4 columns, and so on.
For example:

123 x 72

Step 1
Break the numbers into hundreds, tens and ones and write them along the edges of a grid.

×	100	20	3
70			
2			

Step 2
Multiply each number along the top by each number down the side to complete the grid.

×	100	20	3
70	7,000	1,400	210
2	200	40	6

Step 3
Add the products in each row.

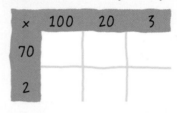

×	100	20	3	
70	7,000	1,400	210	8, 6 1 0
2	200	40	6	+ 2 4 6

Step 4
Add together the totals.   8, 8 5 6

so

123 x 72 = 8,856

Find out more about: digits (page 7); **products** (page 46)

Multiplying with the column method

This method is sometimes called long multiplication. Write the calculation out as shown below, lining up the ones column, then the tens and so on. Multiply the top number by the lowest place value in the bottom number. Then multiply the top number by the next place value, and so on. Add the products together to find the answer. For example:

Step 1

$$3\ 2$$
$$\times\ 2\ 3$$

To multiply 32 and 23, first write them down one above the other with the ones column lined up.

Step 2

$$3\ 2$$
$$\times\ 2\ 3$$
$$\overline{9\ 6}$$

Multiply 32 by 3, starting with the ones column.

$2 \times 3 = 6$
$30 \times 3 = 90$

Step 3

$$3\ 2$$
$$\times\ 2\ 3$$
$$\overline{9\ 6}$$
$$6\ 4\ 0$$

Now multiply 32 by 20.

$2 \times 20 = 40$
$30 \times 20 = 600$
so, 32×20
$= 40 + 600$
$= 640$

Step 4

$$3\ 2$$
$$\times\ 2\ 3$$
$$\overline{9\ 6}$$
$$6\ 4\ 0$$
$$\overline{7\ 3\ 6}$$
$$1$$

Add up the totals.

$96 + 640 = 736$

So, $32 \times 23 = 736$

If the product of two digits is 10 or more, write its ones digit between the lines in the first empty column on the right, and write down the tens below the column next to it. This is often called carrying over. Add the carried over number to the product in the next column, and so on. For example:

$$5\ 6$$
$$\times\ \ 7$$
$$\overline{3\ 9\ 2}$$
$$4$$

$6 \times 7 = 42$
Write the 2 in the ones column and the 4 at the bottom of the tens column.
$5(0) \times 7 = 35(0)$
Add the carried over $4(0)$.
$35(0) + 4(0) = 39(0)$

You can also use the column method to multiply longer whole numbers. For example:

$$1\ 7\ 6$$
$$\times\ \ 3\ 4$$
$$\overline{7\ 0\ 4}$$
$$3\ 2$$
$$5,\ 2\ 8\ 0$$
$$2\ 1$$
$$\overline{5,\ 9\ 8\ 4}$$

3-digit number

$6 \times 4 = 24$, so write the 4 in the ones column and carry the 2 to the tens column, and so on.

The column method works for multiplying decimals, too. For example:

$$3.2 \times 2.1$$

$$3\ 2$$
$$\times\ 2\ 1$$
$$\overline{3\ 2}$$
$$6\ 4\ 0$$
$$\overline{6\ 7\ 2}$$

To multiply decimals, ignore the decimal point. Then put it back in, so that the number of decimal places in the answer is the same as the total number of decimal places in the original numbers.

So $3.2 \ \times \ 2.1 \ = \ 6.72$
$(1\text{ d.p.}) + (1\text{ d.p.}) = (2\text{ d.p.})$

Find out more about: decimals (pages 21-24); **digits** (page 7); **place value** (page 8); **products** (page 46)

Checking multiplication

Always estimate your answer before you do a calculation, and check it afterward. Here are some methods you can use.

Approximating

You can use rounding to get an idea what your result should be, or to check if an answer is sensible. For example, to calculate 41 x 7:

Round down 41 to 40:

$40 \times 7 = 280$
Your answer should be a little larger than 280.

You can use number facts to work out the last digit. For example:

$1 \times 7 = 7$
Your answer should end in a 7.

For a more accurate check, you can round and compensate. For example:

41×7

$= (40 \times 7) + (1 \times 7)$

$= 287$

Rearranging the calculation

You can rearrange the calculation and multiply in a different order, or divide, to check your answer. For example, if 41 x 7 = 287:

$7 \times 41 = 287$

$287 \div 41 = 7$

$287 \div 7 = 41$

> *To remind you which numbers to multiply or divide, you could use a pair of numbers whose relationships you know. For example:*
>
> | | |
> |---|---|
> | $5 \times 3 = 15$ | $a \times b = c$ |
> | $15 \div 3 = 5$ | $c \div b = a$ |
> | $15 \div 5 = 3$ | $c \div a = b$ |

Mental division

Here are several methods for dividing numbers in your head. Before you start, look at the numbers and decide which method you think will work best. If you need to jot down some figures to keep track of your calculations, that's fine.

Dividing by splitting numbers

Split the number you want to divide into, to make numbers that are easier to divide. For example:

$69 \div 3$ *$69 = 60 + 9$*

$60 \div 3 = 20$ *Divide each number by the divisor (here*
$9 \div 3 = 3$ *you divide by 3).*

$20 + 3 = 23$ *Add the answers.*

so $69 \div 3 = 23$

Dividing using factors

Sometimes a calculation is easier if you break up the divisor into its factors, and divide by each one in turn. For example:

$96 \div 6$ *$6 = 3 \times 2$*

$= (96 \div 3) \div 2$

$= 32 \div 2$

$= 16$

$156 \div 12$ *$12 = 3 \times 4$*
    $= 3 \times 2 \times 2$

$= (156 \div 3) \div 2 \div 2$

$= (52 \div 2) \div 2$

$= 26 \div 2$

$= 13$

Find out more about: **brackets** (page 62); **divisors** (page 47); **factors** (pages 11-13); **rounding and compensating in multiplication** (page 55); **times tables** (pages 48-51)

59

Halving even numbers

To divide an even number by another one, halve both numbers (that is, divide them by 2) then keep halving them until the question is simple enough to solve. For example:

$$
\begin{aligned}
112 &\div 28 && (\div 2)\\
= \quad 56 &\div 14 && (\div 2)\\
= \quad 28 &\div 7 && (\div 7)\\
= \quad 4 &\div 1 &&\\
= \quad 4 &&&
\end{aligned}
$$

Dividing by repeated subtraction

Count how many times you can take the smaller number away from the larger one. You might find it helpful to fold down a finger for each subtraction you do. For example, you can take 16 away from 64 four times, so $64 \div 16 = 4$.

Compact division

Writing out the short-hand version of long division counts as mental math, and is called compact division. (You can see how to write out long division in full on page 61.) For example:

$$7{,}752 \div 3$$

$$
\begin{array}{r}
2,5\,8\,4 \\
3\,\overline{)7,{}^1 7 {}^2 5 {}^1 2}
\end{array}
$$

Step 1: 3 into 7 goes twice ($2 \times 3 = 6$).
Carry the remainder 1.
Step 2: 3 into 17 goes 5 times ($5 \times 3 = 15$).
Carry the remainder 2.
Step 3: 3 into 25 goes 8 times ($8 \times 3 = 24$).
Carry the remainder 1.
Step 4: 3 into 12 goes 4 times exactly.

Written division

There are two main ways of writing out division. The one you choose will depend on the numbers you want to divide.

Short division

Short division is a method that works well for dividing by numbers less than 10. Write the calculation out as shown below then divide into each digit in turn, starting with the first digit, and write each result above it. Then read the digits to get the final answer. For example:

$$84 \div 4$$

$$
\begin{array}{r}
2\,1 \\
4\,\overline{)8\,4}
\end{array}
$$

Write each answer along the top of the line:
$8 \div 4 = 2$
$4 \div 4 = 1$
Then read off the numbers to get the final answer: 21.

If you can't divide a digit exactly, write the remainder in front of the next digit and divide into this new number you've made. If you have a remainder at the end of your calculation, include it in your answer.

You can show a final remainder as a whole number, or as a fraction of the divisor. For example, if you have divided by 4 and have a remainder of 2, you could write it as rem. 2, r. 2 or $\frac{1}{2}$ (which is $\frac{2}{4}$ written in its simplest terms). You could also write the fraction as a decimal (in this case, .5). For example:

$$98 \div 4$$

$$
\begin{array}{r}
2\,4 \text{ rem. } 2 \\
4\,\overline{)9\,{}^1 8}
\end{array}
$$

$9 \div 4 = 2$ rem. 1
Write the 1 in front of the 8:
$18 \div 4 = 4$ rem. 2

so $98 \div 4 = 24$ rem. 2

or you can write this as 24 r. 2, $24\frac{1}{2}$ or 24.5.

Find out more about: digits (page 7); **even numbers** (page 9); **subtracting** (pages 35-45)

Long division

Long division is a method that helps you divide by numbers more than 10. You write the calculation down in the same way as short division, then instead of calculating the remainders in your head and "carrying them over," you work them out on paper and "bring down" digits. For example:

$$345 \div 15$$

Step 1

15)3 4 5

15 won't divide into 3, so look at the next digit and divide 34 by 15.

Step 2

$$\begin{array}{r} 2 \\ 15\overline{)3\ 4\ 5} \\ 3\ 0 \\ \hline 4 \end{array}$$

2 x 15 = 30

Write the 2 above the 4. Then take 30 away from 34 to find the remainder.

Step 3

$$\begin{array}{r} 2 \\ 15\overline{)3\ 4\ 5} \\ 3\ 0\downarrow \\ \hline 4\ 5 \end{array}$$

"Bring down" the 5 next to the 4, ready to divide 15 into 45.

Step 4

$$\begin{array}{r} 2\ 3 \\ 15\overline{)3\ 4\ 5} \\ 3\ 0\downarrow \\ \hline 4\ 5 \end{array}$$

3 x 15 = 45

Write the 3 above the 5. There are no more numbers to bring down, so the final answer is 23.

Long division looks harder than it is, and is a reliable way to get accurate answers if you don't have a calculator.

Dividing decimals

You can use both long and short division to divide decimals too. For example:

$$9.3 \div 3$$

9 ÷ 3 = 3
3 ÷ 3 = 1

$$\begin{array}{r} 3\ .\ 1 \\ 3\overline{)9\ .\ 3} \end{array}$$

Write the decimal point in the answer above the decimal point in the question.

Checking division

It's important to estimate the answer before doing a calculation, and then to check it afterward.

Approximating

You can use rounding to give an idea what your result should be, or to check if an answer is sensible. For example, to calculate 148 ÷ 4:

Round up 148 to 150, and round up 4 to 5:

$$150 \div 5 = 30$$

Your answer should be near 30.

Rearranging the calculation

You can rearrange the calculation and check your answer by dividing in a different order, or by multiplying.

For example, if 287 ÷ 7 = 41:

$$287 \div 41 = 7$$
$$7 \times 41 = 287$$
$$41 \times 7 = 287$$

To remind you which numbers to multiply or divide, you could use a pair of numbers whose relationships you know. For example:

5 x 3 = 15	*a x b = c*
15 ÷ 3 = 5	*c ÷ b = a*
15 ÷ 5 = 3	*c ÷ a = b*

Find out more about: decimals (pages 21-24); **rounding** (page 33)

Complex calculations

Many number problems in real life are complicated because you have to do more than one calculation at a time. Here are some tips to help you.

Parentheses

Parentheses are a pair of symbols ( ) that show you which part of a calculation to work out first. For example:

Look at the calculation:

$$4 \times 2 + 3 =$$

There are two ways of doing this but each way gives a different answer. Using parentheses makes it clear what you need to do.

$(4 \times 2) + 3$
$= 8 + 3$
$= 11$

The parentheses tell you to work out 4×2 first. $4 \times 2 = 8$

$4 \times (2 + 3)$
$= 4 \times 5$
$= 20$

The parentheses tell you to work out $2 + 3$ first. $2 + 3 = 5$

Here's another example:

$$16 \div 4 - 3 =$$

$(16 \div 4) - 3$
$= 4 - 3$
$= 1$

The parentheses tell you to work out $16 \div 4$ first. $16 \div 4 = 4$

$16 \div (4 - 3)$
$= 16 \div 1$
$= 16$

The parentheses tell you to work out $4 - 3$ first. $4 - 3 = 1$

Two-part calculations

A two-part calculation has two different operations, such as adding and dividing.

If a calculation only asks you to add and subtract, you can do the calculation in any order. For example, you can do:

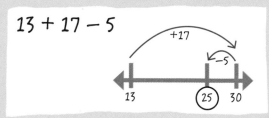

$13 + 17 - 5$

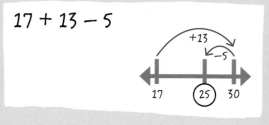

$17 + 13 - 5$

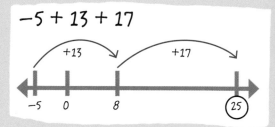

$-5 + 13 + 17$

You put the subtraction sign in front of the 5 to remember that you start the calculation with a negative number.

The answer to all three calculations is the same: 25

$17 - 5 + 13$
is the same as $-5 + 17 + 13$
and $13 + 17 - 5$
and $13 - 5 + 17$
and so on.

62 Find out more about: adding (pages 35-42); dividing (pages 46-61); multiplying (pages 46-59); negative numbers (page 7); subtracting (pages 35-45)

Two-part calculations continued

It doesn't matter how many numbers you need to add and subtract, you can always do them in any order as long as you keep the subtraction signs with the numbers they belong to. For example, you can do:

$$8 - 5 + 10 + 2 - 7$$

or $10 - 5 - 7 + 2 + 8$

or $-5 + 2 + 8 - 7 + 10$

and so on.

and get the same answer (8).
(Use this number line to check.)

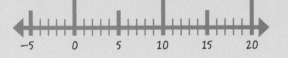

Many-part calculations

When you do a calculation that has two or more parts and includes multiplying or dividing, you have to do the operations in a particular order. This order follows the PEMDAS rule, which has four steps:

Step 1: Parentheses   ( )

Step 2: Exponents a^n

Step 3:
Multiplication or
Division, as it occurs
from left to right   ×
                           ÷

Step 4:
Addition or
Subtraction, as it
occurs from left
to right   +
                           −

An easy way to remember the order is:
Please **E**xcuse **M**y **D**ear **A**unt **S**ally.

Examples of PEMDAS

$$13 + 12 \times 3$$

PEMDAS means doing multiplication before addition, so do:

$13 + (12 \times 3)$
$= 13 + 36$
$= 49$

If you don't use PEMDAS, you get a very different answer:

$(13 + 12) \times 3 = 25 \times 3 = 75$

Here's another example:

$$28 - 14 \div 7 \times 3$$

PEMDAS means doing division, then multiplication, then subtraction, so do:

$28 - (14 \div 7) \times 3$
$= 28 - (2 \times 3)$
$= 28 - 6$
$= 22$

If you don't use PEMDAS, you get very different answers, such as:

$(28 - 14) \div 7 \times 3$
$= (14 \div 7) \times 3$
$= 2 \times 3$
$= 6$

Calculator tip

Beware: some calculators use PEMDAS and some don't. You can find out if your calculator uses PEMDAS by testing it out with the calculations shown in the box above.

Find out more about: adding (pages 35-42); **dividing** (pages 46-61); **multiplying** (pages 46-59); **number lines** (page 8); **subtracting** (pages 35-45)

Using a calculator

The buttons on calculators are keys and you read the answer on the display screen. Here are the main keys you'll see on most calculators.

Digit and decimal point keys

Use these keys to put numbers into the calculator. Some calculators always show a decimal point at the end of whole numbers, even if it has no decimal fractions after it.

The layout and exact selection of keys depends on the model of your calculator, so spend some time getting to know your own model.

Operation keys

These keys divide (÷ or /), multiply (x), subtract (–) or add (+) numbers.

= Equals key

Press this at the end of a calculation to display the answer on the screen. On some calculators you can also use the equals key to do the last operation again*.

For example, $3 + + = = \dots$

(or $3 + = = \dots$ depending on

the model of your calculator) adds 3 to each new total, giving 6, 12, 15, 18 ... You can also start with any number, so

$3 + + 1 0 = = = \dots$

(or $1 0 + 3 + = = \dots$)

gives 13, 16, 19...

CE Clear entry and C Clear

These keys clear or cancel the last key you pressed. This is useful if you make a mistake partway through a calculation.

AC All clear

This key clears all entries and returns the display to 0. Always press this key before you start a new calculation.

√ Square root key

For example, to find the square root of 81, press: $8 \; 1 \; \sqrt{}$.

% Percentage key

You can find out more about using the percentage key on pages 27–28.

A^B/c Fractions key

You can find out more about working with fractions on your calculator on page 19.

*Some calculators have a separate "K" key called a constant key that repeats a function. You will need to play with your own calculator to find out how it works.

Memory keys

You can use the memory keys to store numbers in the calculator's memory and use them in calculations.

 M+ Use this key to save the number on the display in the calculator's memory or to add the number on the display to one you've already stored in the memory.

M− This key subtracts the number on the display from the one stored in the memory.

CM or **MC** This key clears the memory. Always clear the memory before you start a calculation that needs the memory keys.

RM or **MR** or **MRC** This key recalls numbers in the memory onto the display.

You can use the memory keys for calculations with parentheses. For example, (12 × 4) + (20 ÷ 5):

Step 1
Work out the first set of parentheses:

Step 2
The answer (48) will appear on the display. Press *to save it in the memory.*

Step 3
Work out the second set of parentheses:

Step 4
The answer (4) will appear on the display. Add it to the number stored in the memory by pressing *.*

The display will show the result (52).

Not all calculators work the same way, so you may need to press **CE** *between steps 2 and 3.*

+/− **Sign change key**

This key changes a positive number into a negative number and makes a negative one positive. For example, to key in –6, press **6** **+/−** . To make it positive, press **+/−** again.

Recognizing negative numbers

The position of a negative sign on the display depends on the calculator. It might sit just before the number (–6); or just after it (6–). On some calculators, it might be at the far left of the display. To find out where it sits on your calculator display, press **5** **+/−** and see what happens.

Recurring decimals errors

Calculators usually only display eight digits. Some calculations give answers with more than eight digits.

For example, 1 ÷ 3 = shows 0.3333333, but really this answer goes on forever. If you press × 3 = to reverse the calculation, some calculators will show 1, and some will show 0.9999999. One kind of calculator rounds up end digits of 5 or more because it knows that the answer goes on forever. The other kind forgets there are more than eight digits, so you get a smaller number.

Try 2 ÷ 3 = . Some calculators show this as 0.6666667, because they round up. Some show 0.6666666 because they don't. What does your calculator do? If you then do × 3 ÷ 2 = (which is the reverse of 2 ÷ 3 =), you'll get either 1 or 0.9999999.

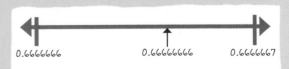

0.66666666 is closer to 0.6666667 than 0.6666666, so your calculator may round it up.

Find out more about: adding (pages 35-42); **decimals** (pages 21-24); **dividing** (pages 46-61); **multiplying** (pages 46-59); **negative numbers, positive numbers** (page 7); **rounding** (page 33); **subtracting** (pages 35-45)

Money and measurements

When you do math with money and measurements you need to make sure that all the amounts in a calculation are in the same units. For example, if you are adding lengths, they should all be in meters, or all be in centimeters, and so on. If you don't, then your answers will be wrong. (You can find out more about changing between units in the measuring section on pages 99-106.)

Once the answer appears on the calculator display, you need to figure out what it means. This will depend what the question was about. Many calculators leave off any final zeros after a decimal point, so you need to think about this too. For example:

Calculating in dollars

Display	Means
6.3	$6.30 or $6 and 30 cents
0.63	$0.63 or 63 cents

You may need to round your answer to two decimal places. For example, round 6.342946 to $6.34.

Calculating in meters

Display	Means
6.3	6.30 meters or 6 meters, 30 centimeters
0.63	0.63 meters or 63 centimeters

You may need to round your answer to two decimal places. For example, 6.342946 becomes 6.34 meters.

Calculating in kilograms

Display	Means
6.3	6.3 kilograms or 6 kilograms, 300 grams
0.63	0.63 kilograms or 630 grams

If the display shows more than three decimal places, you need to round your answer to three decimal places. For example, 6.342946 becomes 6.343 kilograms.

Calculation tips

Calculators do exactly what you ask them to, and they can't tell if you've made a mistake. It's important always to estimate your answer before you do a calculation, so you'll know if the calculator's answer is sensible.

Keep a written record of each calculation as you do it (for example, jot down "468 ÷ 26 = 18,") especially if a question has several stages to it. You can then estimate the result at each stage, to make sure you stay on track for a correct answer.

Always check your answers, too. The quickest way to check a calculation is to do an inverse calculation and see if your answers agree. Remember that addition and subtraction undo each other, and multiplication and division undo each other. For example:

To check $61 \times 12 = 732$

Try $732 \div 12 = 61$

Function machines

A function machine takes in a number as input, does something to it and spits out another number as output. The function can be as simple as adding 1, or it might involve combinations of number operations.

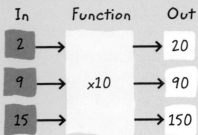

This function machine multiplies the input by 10 to give the output.

Find the output

Some questions tell you the input and the function, and ask you to find the output. To calculate the output you need to apply the function to the input. For example:

In	Function	Out	Working
15	÷3	?	$15 ÷ 3 = 5$
6	x5	?	$6 × 5 = 30$
7	x2 −1	?	$(7 × 2) - 1 = 13$
8	+4 ÷2	?	$(8 + 4) ÷ 2 = 6$

Find the input

To calculate the input, you need to start with the output and apply the opposite, or inverse, of each operation. For example:

In	Function	Out	Working
?	÷3	5	$5 × 3 = 15$
?	x5	30	$30 ÷ 5 = 6$
?	x2 −1	13	$(13 + 1) ÷ 2 = 7$
?	+4 ÷2	6	$(6 × 2) - 4 = 8$

Addition and subtraction are inverse operations. Multiplication and division are inverse operations.

Find the function

Sometimes you will be given the input and the output, and will need to find the function. To do this, look at the input number and see what has been done to it to get the output number. For example:

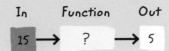

The function could be − 10 or ÷ 3 or any other number of functions.

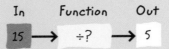

You know it's division, so the function must be ÷3. You would do $15 ÷ 5 = 3$ to find this out.

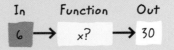

You need to do $30 ÷ 6$ to find the function (x5.)

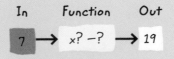

Try possible answers and improve them until the calculation works. 7 x 1 and 7 x 2 are less than 19, so try 7 x 3 (21). Then figure out what you must take from 21 to give 19. The rule could be x3 −2.

Find out more about: adding (pages 35-42); **dividing** (pages 46-61); **multiplying** (pages 46-59); **subtracting** (pages 35-45)

67

Algebra

Algebra is about seeing mathematical patterns, understanding the patterns and describing them using words and symbols. Patterns that are true in lots of different situations are called generalizations.

You can make a generalization about the number of legs in a herd of cows: it is four times the number of cows.

Seeing patterns

You use algebra every day, probably without even noticing. For example:

The total cost of these cars is $6. You could write this as:

A set of 4 cars costs $6.
4 cars cost $6.
4c = $6, where the letter c means cars.

4c means the same as 4 x c, but you avoid using multiplication signs in algebra because they are easily confused with the letter x.

You could draw a table to find out how much one car costs:

Number of cars	Cost	Working
4c	$6	
2c	$3	6 ÷ 2 = 3
c	$1.50	3 ÷ 2 = 1.5

One car costs $1.50.

Think of a number

"Think of a number" is algebra. For example: Think of a number:

?

Double it:

2 x ?

Double it again:

2 x ? x 2 = 4 x ?

Add the number you first thought of:

4 x ? + ? = 5 x ?

Divide by 5, and you get the number you first thought of:

5 x ? ÷ 5 = ?

You can use the letter n instead of a thought bubble to show the number you're thinking of:

This line means "divided by."

4n means "4 multiplied by n."

$$\frac{(2 \times n \times 2) + n}{5} = \frac{4n + n}{5}$$

$$= \frac{5n}{5} = n$$

You can find out more about writing down algebra on page 70.

What's my number?

"What's my number?" is algebra. For example, I'm thinking of a number:

I subtract 1:

$$? - 1$$

I multiply it by 3:

$$(? - 1) \times 3$$

The answer is 15. What's my number?

$$(? - 1) \times 3 = 15$$

You can work backward and undo the operations to find out.

$$(15 \div 3) + 1 = ?$$

I multiplied by 3, so now I divide by 3:

$$15 \div 3 = 5$$

I subtracted 1, so now I add 1:

$$5 + 1 = 6$$

So the number I started with is 6.

You can use the letter n instead of a thought bubble to describe the number you started with:

$$(n - 1) \times 3 = 15$$

Patterns in sequences

Algebra can help you to find terms in number sequences. On page 14 you found out how to calculate the next term in a sequence. But suppose you needed to find the 100th term, or even the 850th term? It would take a very long time to work out all the individual terms one by one. So you need to find the pattern or rule that links the number to its term number (for example, the rule that links the 100th term to the number 100). This is called finding the "nth" term, where the letter n stands for any term number.

For example, here are the first few terms in the sequence of even numbers. The rule for finding the nth term is 2n.

1	2	3	4	5	100
2	4	6	8	10	?

Term 1 is $2 \times 1 = 2$
Term 2 is $2 \times 2 = 4$
Term 3 is $2 \times 3 = 6$
Term 4 is $2 \times 4 = 8$
Term 5 is $2 \times 5 = 10$
Term 100 is $2 \times 100 = 200$

Here are the first few terms in the sequence of odd numbers. The rule for finding the nth term is 2n − 1.

1	2	3	4	5	100
1	3	5	7	9	?

Term 1 is $2 \times 1 - 1 = 1$
Term 2 is $2 \times 2 - 1 = 3$
Term 3 is $2 \times 3 - 1 = 5$
Term 4 is $2 \times 4 - 1 = 7$
Term 5 is $2 \times 5 - 1 = 9$
Term 100 is $2 \times 100 - 1 = 199$

Find out more about: terms in sequences (page 14)

Formulas

You can use a formula to describe a rule that connects two numbers. For example, here is a pattern of purple and blue squares. What will the pattern 10 look like? What will pattern p look like?

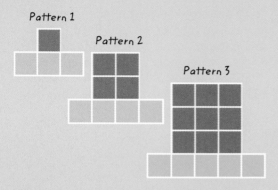

Pattern 1
Pattern 2
Pattern 3

Look at the purple squares first. These go:

Pattern 1   1
Pattern 2   4
Pattern 3   9

They are the square of the number of the pattern. So pattern 10 will have 100 purple squares and pattern p will have p x p or p squared (p^2) purple squares. The formula that describes the rule for finding the number of purple squares is:

$$\text{Purple squares} = p^2$$

Now look at the blue squares. These go:

Pattern 1   3
Pattern 2   4
Pattern 3   5

They are always 2 more than the number of the pattern. So pattern 10 will have 12 blue squares and pattern p will have p + 2 blue squares. The formula for finding the number of blue squares is:

$$\text{Blue squares} = p + 2$$

Tips for writing algebra

A number, letter, or combination of numbers and letters multiplied together is called a term. The terms are separated by + and − signs, and each + or − is "joined" to the term that follows it. Any term that does not have a + or − sign before it is positive. For example:

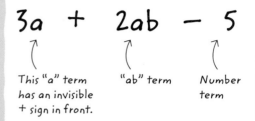

$$3a \quad + \quad 2ab \quad - \quad 5$$

This "a" term has an invisible + sign in front.

"ab" term

Number term

A collection of terms is called an expression. So 3a + 2ab − 5 is an expression.

Here are a few things to remember when you write down expressions:

Write single letters on their own. For example, a is not 1a but just:

a

Avoid using multiplication signs. For example, write "a multiplied by b" as:

ab

Write divisions as fractions, with the divisor on the bottom. For example, write "a divided by b" as:

$\dfrac{a}{b}$

When you multiply numbers and letters, always write the number first. For example, write a x 2 x b as:

$2ab$

Shape and space words

You can describe everything in the world around you, from a dot on a notepad to a soaring skyscraper, in terms of shape and space. Here are some words to help you talk about the shapes you see.

Points

A point is a place. It has no length, width or thickness and you usually show a point on diagrams by a dot or an x. You can describe the position of a point by giving its coordinates (see page 92).

✗   ● Dot and x showing points

Lines and line segments

A line segment joins two points on a line. In the world of math, a line itself goes on forever in both directions, but in everyday life, most people describe a line segment as a line too. For example:

Line   Line segment

Point   Point

The purple line segment is part of the longer green line. The arrows on the ends of the line show it goes on forever.

Angles

An angle is the amount of turn between two lines, measured in degrees (°). You can find out more about angles on pages 94-97.

Parallel lines

Parallel lines are the same distance apart all the way along. They never meet, no matter how long they are.

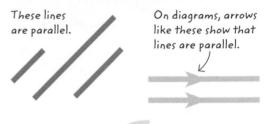

These lines are parallel.

On diagrams, arrows like these show that lines are parallel.

Parallel lines can be straight or curved.

Perpendicular lines

Lines that are perpendicular are at right angles to each other. Lines don't have to touch to be perpendicular.

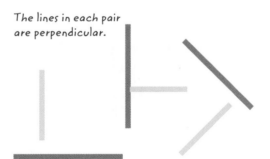

The lines in each pair are perpendicular.

Each purple line is perpendicular to its green line, and each green line is perpendicular to its purple one.

Symmetry

A shape has symmetry if you can halve it or turn it so that it fits exactly onto itself. You can read more about symmetry on pages 85-87.

Find out more about: right angles (page 94)

2-D shapes

Pictures of shapes on paper or cardboard are called two-dimensional shapes, or 2-D shapes for short. This means they have length and width, but no thickness. Another name for a 2-D shape is a plane, or plane figure.

These shapes are 2-dimensional. 2-D shapes can have straight or curved edges, or a mixture of the two.

Polygons

Any 2-D shape with straight sides is called a polygon. There are lots of different polygons. What makes one polygon different from (or the same as) another is the number of sides it has, and the angles formed by their edges. Here are some useful polygon words you need to know:

Vertices

Each corner of a polygon, where two sides meet, is called a vertex. The plural is vertices (say "vurty-sees.")

Vertex

This shape is a hexagon. It has six vertices.

Sides

The line between two vertices of a shape is a side.

Side

A triangle has three sides.

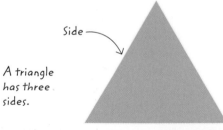

Included angles

Angles inside a polygon (at the vertices) are called included angles or interior angles.

All the interior angles in a square are right angles (90°).

Diagonals

A diagonal is a line that joins two vertices that are not next to each other. Diagonals can be inside or outside of a polygon.

These diagonals are inside the polygon.

This diagonal is outside the polygon.

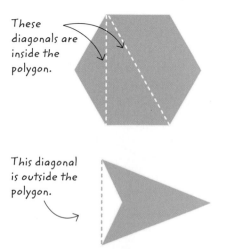

Regular polygons

All the sides in a regular polygon are the same length, and all the angles are the same size. For example, these shapes are all regular polygons:

Equilateral triangle

Square

Regular pentagon

Regular hexagon

Equiangular polygons

All the angles in an equiangular polygon are equal, but the sides don't all have to be the same length.

This rectangle is an equiangular polygon.

Equilateral polygons

All the sides in an equilateral polygon are the same length. Its angles don't have to be equal.

This shape is called a rhombus. It is an equilateral polygon.

Irregular polygons

In an irregular polygon, the sides and angles are not all the same. Here are some examples of irregular polygons:

Irregular triangle

Irregular quadrilateral

Irregular pentagon

Irregular hexagon

Convex polygons

In a convex polygon all the included angles are less than 180° (degrees).

All the angles in a convex polygon are acute angles (less than 90°) or obtuse angles (between 90° and 180°).

Concave polygons

A concave polygon has at least one included angle that is more than 180°.

One of the angles in this polygon is more than 180°, so the shape is a concave polygon.

Find out more about: angles (pages 94-97); **degrees** (page 94)

Naming polygons

Polygons get their names from the number of angles and sides they have. The first part of their name is from the Greek (or sometimes Latin) word for the number. Most polygon names end in "...gon." This comes from the Greek word for "knee," or angle.

For example, the Greek for six is "hexa" so a hexagon is a shape with six angles. Shapes always have the same number of sides as angles, so you know from its name that a hexagon has six sides too.

Polyhedrons are named in a similar way. The "hedron" part comes from the Greek word for faces. You can find out more about polyhedra on pages 81-83.

Word	Language	Number
tri	Greek	3
quad	Latin	4
tetra	Greek	4
penta	Greek	5
hexa	Greek	6
hepta	Greek	7
septa	Latin	7
octa	Greek and Latin	8
nona	Greek	9
deca	Greek	10
hendeca	Greek	11
dodeca	Greek	12
icosa	Greek	20

Some common polygons

Here are the polygons you'll see most often. The ones below are regular. (A regular polygon has sides and angles that are the same length and size.) Irregular polygons have the same number of sides and angles as regular ones, but the lengths and sizes vary.

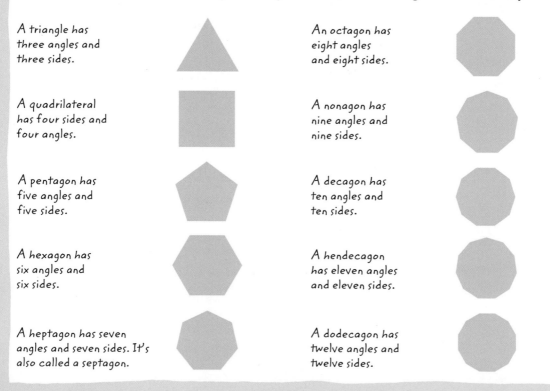

A triangle has three angles and three sides.

A quadrilateral has four sides and four angles.

A pentagon has five angles and five sides.

A hexagon has six angles and six sides.

A heptagon has seven angles and seven sides. It's also called a septagon.

An octagon has eight angles and eight sides.

A nonagon has nine angles and nine sides.

A decagon has ten angles and ten sides.

A hendecagon has eleven angles and eleven sides.

A dodecagon has twelve angles and twelve sides.

Triangles

There are several different types of triangles. All triangles have three angles and three sides. The top vertex of a triangle is called the apex. The side it sits on is the base.

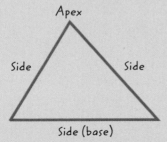

Apex

Side   Side

Side (base)

Right-angled triangles

A right-angled triangle contains one right angle (90°).

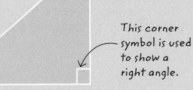

This corner symbol is used to show a right angle.

Equilateral triangles

An equilateral triangle has three equal angles and three equal sides. It is sometimes called a regular triangle.

Angles a, b and c are all 60°. You can work this out because the angles of a triangle add up to 180° and an equilateral triangle has three equal angles.
180° ÷ 3 = 60°

Sides x, y and z are the same length.

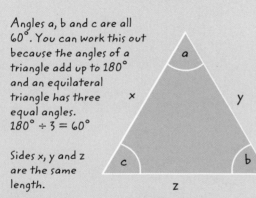

a

x   y

c   b

z

Isosceles triangles

An isosceles triangle has two equal angles and two equal sides. "Isosceles" is a Greek word that means "equal legs."

Angles a and b are equal, and sides x and y are equal.

The symbols // show which sides are equal.

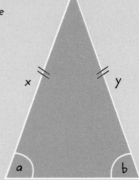

x   y

a   b

Isosceles triangles can be right-angled, like this one, but they don't have to be.

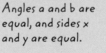

Scalene triangles

A scalene triangle has no equal sides and no equal angles.

No equal sides
No equal angles

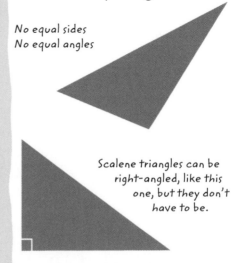

Scalene triangles can be right-angled, like this one, but they don't have to be.

Find out more about: angles (pages 94-97); **angles in a triangle** (page 97); **right angles** (page 94); **sides** (page 72)

Quadrilaterals

"Quad" is a Latin word that means "four," and quadrilaterals are polygons that have four sides and four angles. These pages show you some important quadrilaterals to look for.

Parallelograms

In a parallelogram, sides that are opposite each other are equal and parallel, and the angles opposite each other are equal.

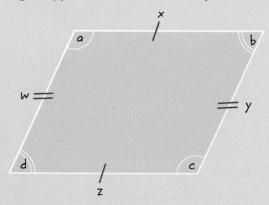

Sides w and y are equal and parallel, and sides x and z are equal and parallel. The opposite angles of this parallelogram are equal too (a = c and b = d), and it doesn't have any right angles.

Rectangles

A rectangle has two pairs of equal sides and four right angles. Rectangles are a type of parallelogram and are sometimes called oblongs.

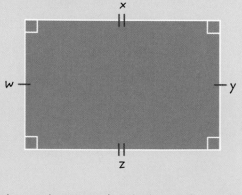

Sides w and y are equal, and sides x and z are equal. All the angles are right angles.

Squares

A square is a special type of rectangle that has four equal sides and four right angles.

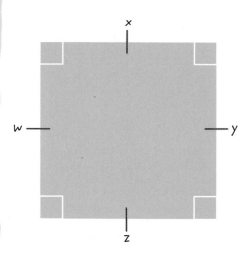

Sides w, x, y and z are the same length, and all the angles are 90°.

The opposite sides of a square are parallel, and its diagonals are the same length as each other.

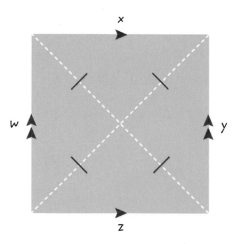

Sides w and y are parallel and sides x and z are parallel.

If you cut a square in half across a diagonal, you make two right-angled isosceles triangles.

Rhombuses

A rhombus is a parallelogram, which means its opposite sides are parallel. Its sides are all the same length, and opposite angles are equal, but it has no right angles.

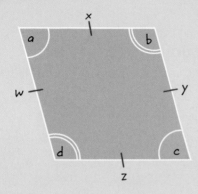

Sides w and y are parallel and sides x and z are parallel. The opposite angles are equal (a = c, and b = d).

A rhombus standing on its vertex, like this, is sometimes called a diamond.

Trapezoids

A trapezoid is a quadrilateral that has only one pair of parallel sides.

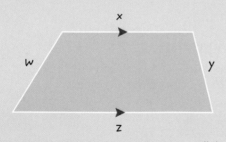

The arrows show that sides x and z are parallel.

An isosceles trapezoid has two pairs of sides that are the same length.

Kites

A kite has two pairs of equal adjacent sides. Adjacent means that they are next to each other. One pair of opposite angles is also equal.

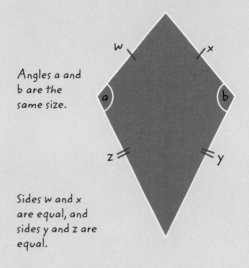

Angles a and b are the same size.

Sides w and x are equal, and sides y and z are equal.

Arrowheads

Like a kite, an arrowhead also has two pairs of equal adjacent sides. One included angle is a reflex angle, which means it's greater than 180°. Another name for an arrowhead is a delta.

Lines w and x are equal, and lines y and z are equal.

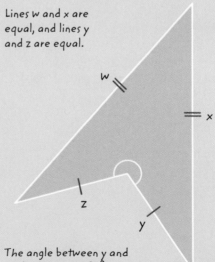

The angle between y and z is larger than 180°.

Find out more about: included angles (page 72); **parallel lines** (page 71); **sides** (page 72); **vertex** (vertices) (page 72)

Circles

A circle is a flat round shape made by a single curved line. Every point on the edge of a circle is exactly the same distance from the middle. Several parts of a circle have their own names.

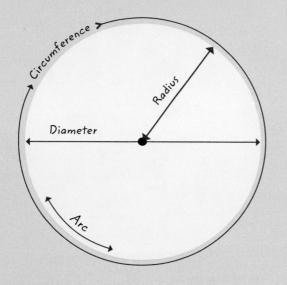

Radius

A radius is a straight line from the middle of a circle to a point on its edge. The plural of radius is radii (say "ray-dee-eye.") A radius is half as long as a diameter.

Diameters

A diameter is a straight line through the middle of a circle that joins two points on its edge. A diameter is twice as long as a radius.

Circumferences

A circle's circumference is the total distance around the edge.

Arcs

An arc is a part of the circumference.

Semicircles

A semicircle is half a circle.

The straight line in a semicircle is a diameter.

Quadrants

A quarter of a circle is called a quadrant.

The radii in a quadrant always form a right angle (90°).

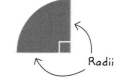

Radii

Sectors

A sector is part of a circle formed by an arc and two radii.

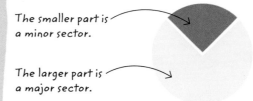

The smaller part is a minor sector.

The larger part is a major sector.

Chords

A chord is a straight line that joins any two points on a circle. (A diameter is a chord that goes through the middle of the circle.)

Segments

The parts of a circle on either side of a chord are called segments.

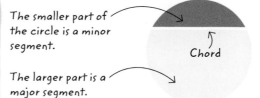

The smaller part of the circle is a minor segment.

Chord

The larger part is a major segment.

Concentric circles

Concentric circles are circles of different sizes that have the same center point.

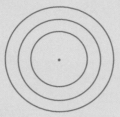

These circles are concentric.

Overlapping circles

When circles overlap, part of one circle covers part of another one.

These circles are overlapping.

Pi

Pi is a special number you can use to find the circumference of a circle. The symbol for Pi is π, which is the letter "p" in the Greek alphabet. Pi has an infinite number of decimal places. When you are using it in a calculation, you use $\frac{22}{7}$, or 3.142. To find a circle's circumference, multiply its diameter (or twice the radius) by π. For example:

If a circle's diameter is 10 inches, its circumference is:

$$3.142 \times 10 = 31.42 \text{ inches}$$

You can write the rule using algebra (with letters standing for numbers):

> $Circumference = 2\pi r$
> or $Circumference = \pi d$
>
> *This stands for:*
> *Circumference = 2 × π × radius*
> *or Circumference = π × diameter*

Ellipses

An ellipse is a squashed or flattened circle. Points on the circumference of an ellipse are different distances from the middle.

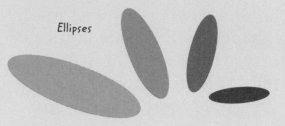

Ellipses

Drawing circles and arcs

The easiest way to draw a circle or an arc is to draw around something round, such as a jelly-jar lid or a plate. You can also use a pair of compasses like the one shown here.

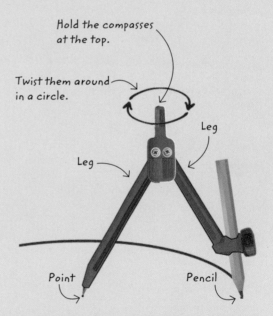

Hold the compasses at the top.

Twist them around in a circle.

Leg

Leg

Point

Pencil

Pull the legs of the compasses apart, then put the point on a piece of paper and swing the compasses around. Make sure you keep the point and the pencil tip on the paper all the time.

To draw a circle, swing the compasses around a whole turn. Swing them just a little way to draw an arc.

Find out more about: algebra (pages 68-70); decimal places (page 22)

Combining shapes

A pattern of shapes that fit together without leaving any gaps is a tessellation. Shapes that tessellate fit together in this way. Many shapes tessellate, though not all do. There are two kinds of tessellation that use only regular polygons.

Jigsaws puzzles are made up of tessellating shapes.

These squares tessellate.

These circles don't tessellate.

Any quadrilaterals tessellate.

Semi-regular tessellations

Semi-regular tessellations use more than one kind of regular polygon. There are eight semi-regular tessellations. These use a mix of equilateral triangles, squares, hexagons, octagons and dodecagons.

Octagons and squares

Dodecagons and equilateral triangles

Hexagons and equilateral triangles

Hexagons, squares and equilateral triangles

Hexagons and equilateral triangles

Hexagons, squares and dodecagons

Regular tessellations

A regular tessellation uses just one kind of regular polygon.

There are only three polygons that make regular tessellations: equilateral triangles, squares and hexagons.

Equilateral triangles

Squares

Hexagons

Squares and equilateral triangles

Squares and equilateral triangles

80 Find out more about: **dodecagons** (page 74); **equilateral triangles** (page 75); **hexagons** (page 74); **octagons** (page 74); **polygons** (pages 72-77); **quadrilaterals** (pages 76-77); **squares** (page 76)

3-D shapes

A three-dimensional (or 3-D) shape is anything that has length, width and thickness. 3-D things can be solid or hollow and can be any shape or size. For example, both a balloon and a brick have 3-D shapes. 3-D shapes may have one or all of the following parts:

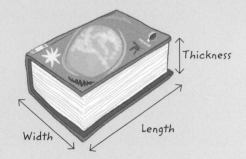

A book has length, width and thickness, so it is 3-dimensional.

Faces

A surface of a 3-D shape is called a face. The face a shape sits on is its base. Faces can be flat or curved.

A cube has flat faces.

A sphere's face is curved.

Edges

The edge is the line where two faces of a 3-D shape meet.

Vertices

A vertex is a point on a 3-D shape where three or more of its faces meet. Vertices (say "vurty-sees") is the plural. The top vertex is an apex.

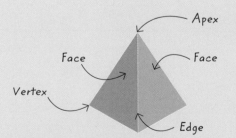

Cross sections

A cross section is a flat surface you make by cutting straight across through a solid.

The cross section of a rectangular pyramid is a rectangle.

Polyhedrons

A polyhedron is a 3-D shape whose surface is made up of polygons. The plural word is polyhedrons or polyhedra. Here are the names of some common polyhedrons. These names come from the Greek number words on page 74.

Name of polyhedron	Number of faces
Tetrahedron	4
Pentahedron	5
Hexahedron	6
Heptahedron	7
Octahedron	8
Nonahedron	9
Decahedron	10
Dodecahedron	12
Icosahedron	20

Find out more about: rectangles (page 76)

Regular polyhedrons

The faces of a regular polyhedron are regular polygons of the same shape and size. For example, all the faces of a cube are squares. There are five regular polyhedrons:

A regular tetrahedron has four faces that are equilateral triangles.

A cube has six square faces.

A regular octahedron has eight faces that are equilateral triangles.

A regular dodecahedron has 12 faces, all pentagons.

A regular icosahedron has 20 faces that are equilateral triangles.

Semi-regular polyhedrons

The faces of a semi-regular polyhedron are more than one shape of regular polygons.

An icosidodecahedron is a semi-regular polyhedron with 32 faces. 20 faces are triangles; the other 12 are pentagons.

Pyramids

A pyramid is a polyhedron with triangular sides that meet at a point. The base of a pyramid is a polygon. If this is a regular polygon, the pyramid is a regular pyramid.

A triangle pyramid has a triangle for its base. If all its sides are equilateral triangles, like the blue polyhedron on the left, the pyramid is a tetrahedron.

A square pyramid has a square base.

The base of a pentagonal pyramid is a pentagon.

Cones

A cone has a curved surface that reaches a point. Its base is a circle.

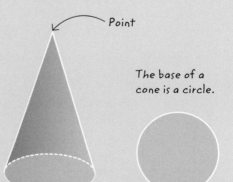

Point

The base of a cone is a circle.

Find out more about: **circles** (pages 78-79); **equilateral triangles** (page 75); **pentagons** (page 74); **polyhedrons** (page 81); **regular polygons** (page 73); **squares** (page 76)

Prisms

A prism is a polyhedron that has two faces the same shape that are parallel to each other. (Parallel faces are the same distance from each other all the way along.) All the other faces are rectangles. Any shape can form the base of a prism. For example:

All the faces of a cuboid are rectangles.

A cube is a cuboid that has square faces. (Remember, a square is a special type of rectangle, which is why a cube is a prism.)

The end faces of a triangular prism are triangles.

The end faces of a cylinder are circles.

The end faces of this prism are star-shaped. It's an irregular decahedral prism.

The flat face you make by cutting through a solid is called a cross section. If you cut a prism into slices, all its cross sections are the same shape and size.

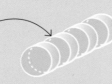

Cross section of a cylinder

Spheres

A sphere is a perfectly round solid. Its cross sections are circles. A shape like this is spherical.

A sphere has one face.

Hemispheres

A hemisphere is half a sphere. Its base is a circle.

A hemisphere has two faces.

Elevations

An elevation is a 2-D drawing of a 3-D solid.

Solid

If you look at an object from the front, the view you see is a front elevation.

Front elevation

A side elevation is what you see if you look at an object from the side.

Side elevation

Plans

If you look at a solid from above, the view you see is called a plan.

Plan

Find out more about: 2-D shapes (page 72); **faces** (page 81); **polyhedrons** (page 81); **rectangles** (page 76)

Nets

A net is a 2-D shape that you can fold to make a 3-D solid. Some solids can have more than one net.

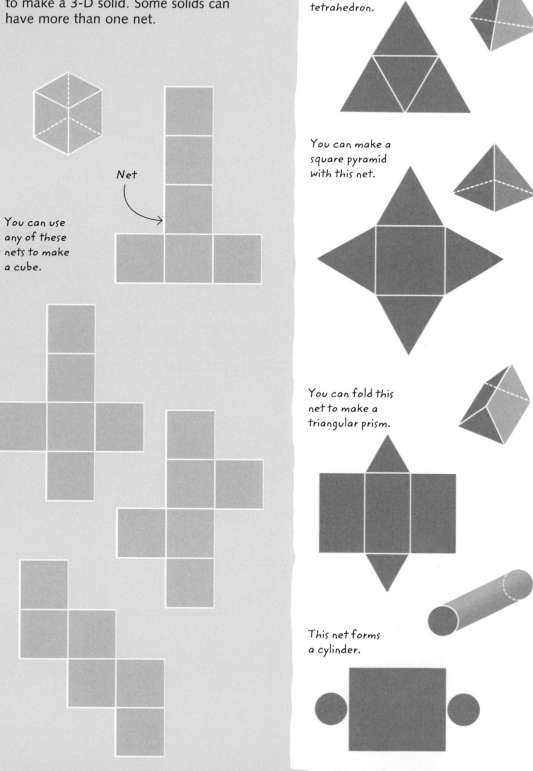

Net

You can use any of these nets to make a cube.

This net makes a regular tetrahedron.

You can make a square pyramid with this net.

You can fold this net to make a triangular prism.

This net forms a cylinder.

Find out more about: cubes (page 82); **cylinders** (page 83); **regular tetrahedrons** (page 82); **square pyramids** (page 82); **triangular prisms** (page 83)

Symmetry

Many shapes have symmetry, which means you can divide them in half or turn them around so they fit exactly onto themselves. A shape or solid that is not symmetric is asymmetric. There are two types of symmetry: reflection and rotation.

Snowflakes are symmetrical. One half is an exact match of the other.

Mirror symmetry, reflection symmetry or line symmetry

If a shape has mirror symmetry, you can divide it into two matching half-shapes. Other names for mirror symmetry are reflection symmetry and line symmetry. Each half-shape is a reflection of the other one. For example:

If you put a mirror next to this half-butterfly shape, the shape and the reflection make a picture of a whole butterfly.

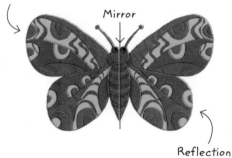

Mirror

Reflection

If you put a mirror next to this half-house shape, the shape and the reflection make a picture of a whole house.

Mirror   Reflection

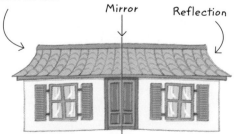

Mirror lines or lines of symmetry

A line that divides a shape in half to give two matching half-shapes is called a mirror line or a line of symmetry. It may be a real line drawn onto a shape, or an imaginary line.

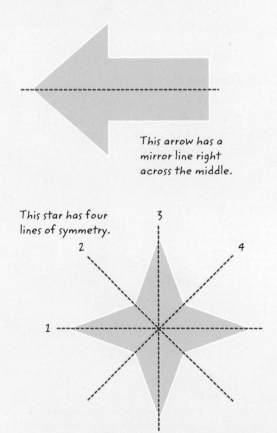

This arrow has a mirror line right across the middle.

This star has four lines of symmetry.

85

Rotational symmetry

If a shape has rotational symmetry, you can turn it around a point to fit exactly onto itself. For example:

Turning this shape means that you can fit each part onto the other part. You could trace the shape onto tracing paper and try this out for yourself.

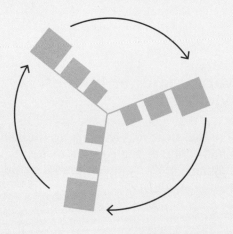

Order of rotational symmetry

A shape's order of rotational symmetry is the number of times in a full turn (360°) that it fits exactly onto itself.

This star shape can fit onto itself four times, so it has rotational symmetry of order 4.

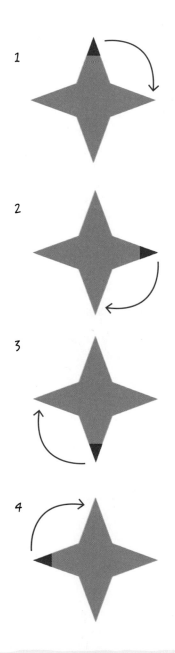

Center of rotational symmetry

The point a shape turns around to fit exactly onto itself is its center of rotational symmetry.

The red dot in the middle of this star shows its center of rotational symmetry.

If you trace the star onto a piece of paper and stick a pin in the center of rotation, you can turn the paper star around to fit exactly onto this one.

Symmetry in 2-D shapes

Equilateral triangles
3 lines of symmetry
Order of rotational
symmetry: 3

Isosceles triangles
1 line of symmetry
Order of rotational
symmetry: 1

Squares
4 lines of symmetry
Order of rotational
symmetry: 4

Rectangles
2 lines of symmetry
Order of rotational
symmetry: 2

Rhombuses
2 lines of symmetry
Order of rotational
symmetry: 2

Kites
1 line of symmetry
Order of rotational
symmetry: 1

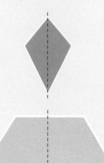

Isosceles trapezoids
1 line of symmetry
Order of rotational
symmetry: 1

Arrowheads
1 line of symmetry
Order of rotational
symmetry: 1

Pentagons
5 lines of symmetry
Order of rotational
symmetry: 5

Hexagons
6 lines of symmetry
Order of rotational
symmetry: 6

Heptagons
7 lines of symmetry
Order of rotational
symmetry: 7

Octagons
8 lines of symmetry
Order of rotational
symmetry: 8

Nonagons
9 lines of symmetry
Order of rotational
symmetry: 9

Decagons
10 lines of symmetry
Order of rotational
symmetry: 10

Hendecagons
11 lines of symmetry
Order of rotational
symmetry: 11

Dodecagons
12 lines of symmetry
Order of rotational
symmetry: 12

Ellipses
2 lines of symmetry
Order of rotational
symmetry: 2

Circles
Infinite lines of symmetry
Order of rotational
symmetry: infinite

Find out more about: circles (pages 78-79); **four-sided shapes** (pages 76-77); **ellipses** (page 79); **infinity** (page 7); **shapes with more than four sides** (page 74); **triangles** (page 75)

Moving shapes and solids

You can change a shape or solid by moving it or making it bigger or smaller. This is called transformation. The original shape or solid is called the object and the new one is the image. Three types of transformation are reflection, rotation and translation.

Clockwise and counterclockwise

If something moves clockwise, it goes around to the right, like the hands of a clock. The opposite way is counterclockwise.

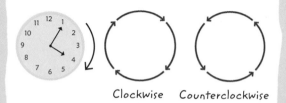

Clockwise   Counterclockwise

Rotation

If you rotate an object, you turn it around a fixed point, called the center of rotation. You can rotate an object clockwise or counterclockwise, but the object and its image always stay the same distance from the center of rotation.

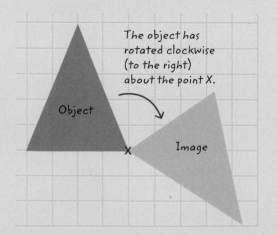

The object has rotated clockwise (to the right) about the point X.

Object

Image

X

Step 1
To rotate a shape, trace it onto tracing paper and lay your trace so it fits over the object.

Step 2
Put your pencil on the center of rotation, and turn the tracing paper. For example, to rotate the shape below a quarter turn clockwise around the point X, twist the tracing paper a quarter turn to the right.

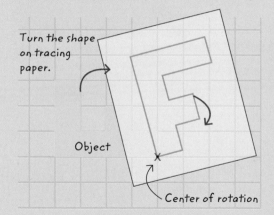

Turn the shape on tracing paper.

Object

Center of rotation

Step 3
Mark a dot where each corner of the shape now sits.

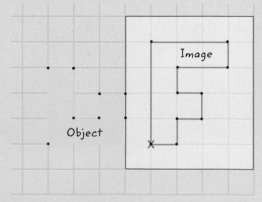

Image

Object

X

Step 4
Join the dots to show the position of the image.

Reflection

When you reflect an object, you "flip" it, so that each point on the image is the same distance away from an imaginary mirror (called a mirror line) as the original.

This object has been reflected in the mirror line.

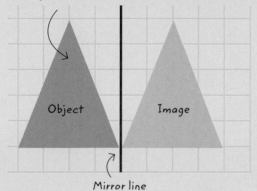

Mirror line

Step 1
To draw a reflection, mark each important point on the shape with a dot.

Step 2
Count the squares from a dot to the mirror line. Then count the same number of squares on the other side of the mirror line and draw another dot. Repeat this step for each dot on the object.

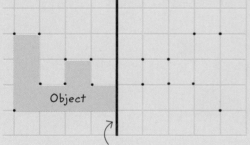

Object

Mirror line

Step 3
Join the dots together to make the image. You could put a small mirror on the line to check your drawing.

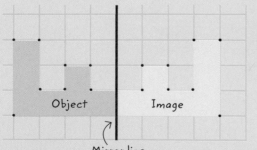

Mirror line

Translation

Sliding an object into a new position without flipping or turning it is called translation. The object and the translated image look the same but they are different distances from a fixed point. Translation is a combination of sliding to the left or right, then sliding up or down.

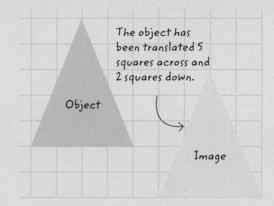

The object has been translated 5 squares across and 2 squares down.

Object

Image

Step 1
To translate a shape, choose an important point on it, such as a corner. Count the number of squares you want to move it across and then the number of squares up or down to find its new position.

Step 2
Count out the new position of other important points in the same way until you have a mark showing the position of each new point.

Step 3
Join the marks together to draw the image.

For example, to move this object 5 places right and 3 up:

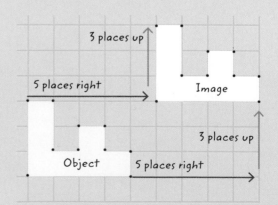

3 places up

5 places right

Image

3 places up

Object

5 places right

Find out more about: points (page 71); **mirror lines** (page 85)

Congruent shapes

If shapes are congruent, it means they are exactly the same shape and size as each other, but are in a different position. Two shapes are congruent if you can cut one out and turn, flip or move it to fit exactly on top of the other one. Rotation, reflection and translation make congruent shapes.

These shapes are congruent – they are all the same shape and size.

Enlargement

Changing the size of an object but not its shape is called enlargement. The amount you enlarge an object is its scale factor. If the scale factor is positive, then the image is larger than the object. If the scale factor is negative, the image is smaller than the object. For example, a scale factor of 2 makes the image twice the size of the object. A scale factor of −2 makes the image half the size of the object.

Step 1
To enlarge a shape, measure it and multiply each measurement by the scale factor to find out what the new measurements should be.

Step 2
Then draw your new shape.

For example, to enlarge this triangle by a scale factor of 2:

Base of object = 2 squares
Base of image = 2 × 2 = 4 squares

Height of object = 3 squares
Height of image = 2 × 3
= 6 squares

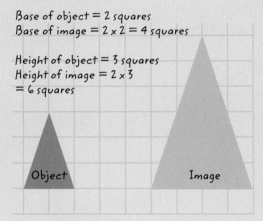

To enlarge this triangle by a scale factor of −2:

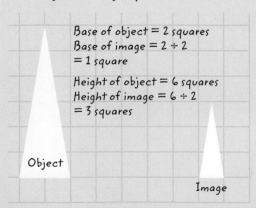

Base of object = 2 squares
Base of image = 2 ÷ 2
= 1 square

Height of object = 6 squares
Height of image = 6 ÷ 2
= 3 squares

Find out more about: bases of triangles (page 75); **negative numbers** (page 7); **positive numbers** (page 7); **reflection** (page 89); **rotation** (page 88); **translation** (page 89)

Position and direction

It's often difficult to describe where something is without talking about something else. To see how hard it is, try explaining exactly where you are at the moment without using words like "near," "in" or "on." In math you can describe the position of things using a grid of squares called a coordinate grid.

Horizontal

The horizon is the line where the earth and the sky seem to meet, and something horizontal lies level with the horizon. A line on a page is a drawing, so it isn't truly horizontal, because it depends how you hold the book. But people have agreed to describe a line drawn straight across a page as horizontal.

This picture shows you what things look like when they're horizontal.

The green line represents the horizon.

Vertical

Something that is at right angles to the horizon is vertical. A line on a page is a drawing, so it isn't truly vertical, because it depends how you hold the book. But people have agreed to describe a line drawn straight down a page as vertical.

This picture shows you what things look like when they're vertical.

The green line represents the horizon.

Right angle

Oblique

Something that is not horizontal or vertical is oblique. People often use the word diagonal too.

This picture shows you what things look like when they're oblique.

The green line represents the horizon.

Coordinate grids

A coordinate grid has two important lines called axes (say "ak-sees"), which have numbers on them. The x-axis is horizontal and the y-axis is vertical. The point where the two axes meet is called the origin. Its coordinates are (0, 0). Marking a point on a grid is called plotting a point.

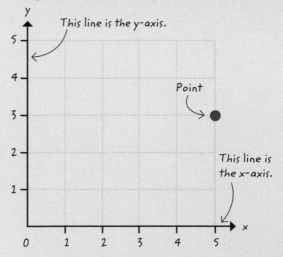

This line is the y-axis.

Point

This line is the x-axis.

Find out more about: coordinates (page 92); **points** (page 71); **right angles** (page 94)

Coordinates

Coordinates are a pair of numbers that describes the position of a point on a grid. To find a point's coordinates, you need to look at the numbers of the lines it sits on.

First look at the number of the line along the x-axis, and next the number of the line up the y-axis. Then write the coordinates in parentheses with a comma between the numbers, like this: (x, y). Always write the x-axis number first. This is easy to remember, because x comes before y in the alphabet. Or you could use the story "The three bears went into the house and up the stairs," to help you remember.

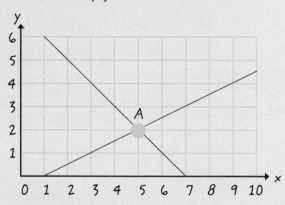

For example, point A sits on line 5 on the x-axis and line 2 on the y-axis, so its coordinates are (5, 2). (You'd say "five-two.")

$$A = (5, 2)$$

x-coordinates

The x-coordinate is the number that shows the position of a point along the x-axis. The x-coordinate of point A above is 5.

y-coordinates

The y-coordinate is the number that shows the position of a point on the y-axis. The y-coordinate of point A above is 2.

Negative coordinates

A point that has negative coordinates sits behind or below the axes. For example, points A, C and D have negative coordinates:

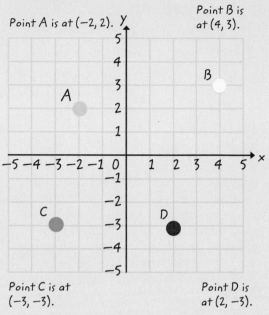

Point A is at (−2, 2).

Point B is at (4, 3).

Point C is at (−3, −3).

Point D is at (2, −3).

Quadrants

The four areas on a grid formed by the axes are quadrants. For example:

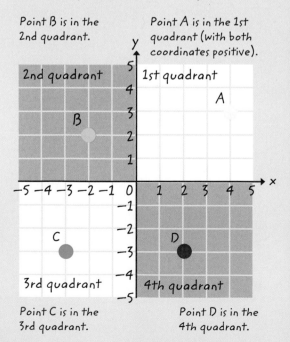

Point B is in the 2nd quadrant.

Point A is in the 1st quadrant (with both coordinates positive).

Point C is in the 3rd quadrant.

Point D is in the 4th quadrant.

Patterns of coordinates

If the lines that join points form a pattern (such as a curve or a straight line), then the coordinates have a pattern too.

For example, the points on the grid below lie on a straight line. Their coordinates are (2, 1), (4, 2), (6, 3) and (8, 4). If you compare the numbers in each pair, you can see that each y-coordinate is half of the x-coordinate. Point (10, 5) will also lie on this line because it follows the pattern (5 = 10 ÷ 2). The point (7, 5) won't lie on the line because it doesn't follow the pattern.

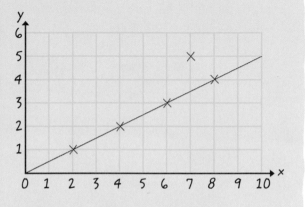

Intersecting lines

Lines that cross each other are called intersecting lines. If the lines are on a grid, you can give the coordinate of the point where they cross, or intersect.

For example, these two lines intersect at the point (5, 2).

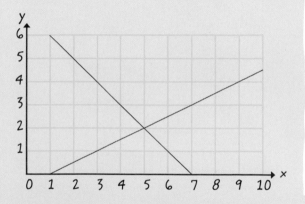

Points of the compass

A compass is an instrument you use for measuring direction. If you hold a compass flat, it points to the north, and you can use that to work out other directions.

The four main compass points (or directions) are north (N) at the top, south (S) at the bottom, east (E) on the right and west (W) on the left. A useful way to remember which is east and west, is that their first letters spell "we."

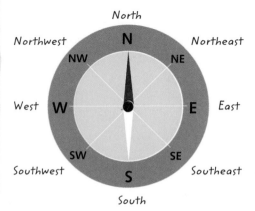

Between these are northeast (NE), southeast (SE), southwest (SW) and northwest (NW).

You can use compass points to give directions, or describe the position of places. For example, on the grid below, the witches' cave is east of the haunted house but south of the wizard's castle.

Find out more about: lines (page 71); points (page 71)

Angles

An angle is the amount of turn between two lines joined at a vertex. The measure of an angle is the amount that you would need to turn one line to sit exactly on top of the other one. The lines on either side of the angle are called arms.

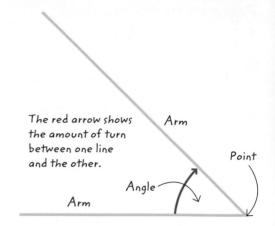

The red arrow shows the amount of turn between one line and the other.

Arm

Point

Angle

Arm

Degrees

You measure angles in degrees and the symbol for degrees is °. For example:

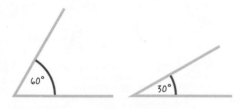

60°

30°

The sizes of these angles are just shown by the numbers, but some angles have special names that tell you about their size.

Straight angles

180°, or half a full turn is called a straight angle or a flat angle.

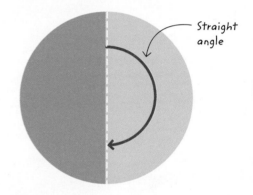

Straight angle

Full turns

A full turn is when a line turns around 360 degrees in a complete circle. There are 360° in a full turn, because people used to think it took 360 days for the Earth to do a full trip around the Sun.

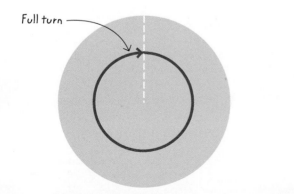

Full turn

Right angles

A right angle is a quarter of a full turn. It measures 90°.

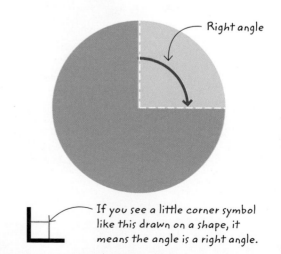

Right angle

If you see a little corner symbol like this drawn on a shape, it means the angle is a right angle.

Acute angles

Any angle smaller than a right angle (90°) is an acute angle.

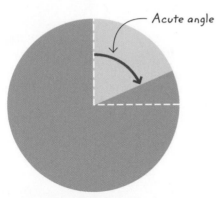

Acute angle

Obtuse angles

An obtuse angle is bigger than a right angle (90°), but smaller than a straight angle (180°).

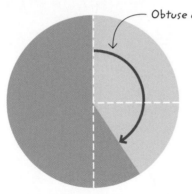

Obtuse angle

Reflex angles

A reflex angle is bigger than a straight angle (180°).

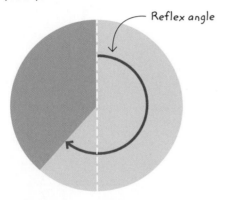

Reflex angle

Estimating angles

To measure whether an angle is more or less than a right angle, just tear off a corner of paper and place it over the angle to compare it.

This angle is more than a right angle.

Corner of paper

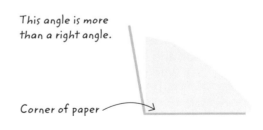

This angle is less than a right angle.

You can also fold the paper in half to estimate 45 degree angles.

This angle is more than 45°.

Corner folded in two

This angle is less than 45°.

To estimate 30 degree angles, fold the corner of the piece of paper into three.

This angle is about 30°.

Corner folded in three

This angle is less than 30°.

Using protractors

You can use a protractor to measure and draw angles. Protractors come in two shapes, semicircles and circles, but you use them both in a similar way.

To measure an angle, lay the cross mark in the middle of the protractor on the point where the angle's arms meet. Line up one of the zeros on the scale with one arm of the angle. See where its other arm touches the scale and read the measurement.

Remember always to estimate an angle's size before you measure it. That way, you will know if your reading is sensible.

To draw an angle with a protractor, use a ruler to draw a straight line. Lay your protractor on the line, with the cross mark at the end of the line where you want to draw your angle. Use the scale that starts at 0 on your line, measure the angle you want, and make a small pencil mark on the paper.

You can use this set of markings to measure angles up to 360°.

These markings measure up to 90° whichever way an angle's arms open out.

This angle measures 45°.

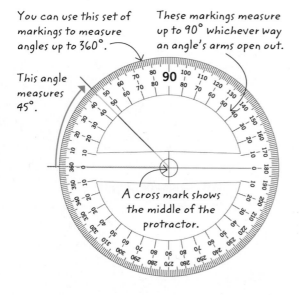

A cross mark shows the middle of the protractor.

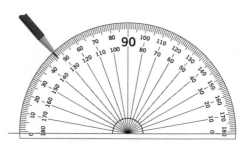

Use a ruler to draw a straight line between the mark and the end of the line.

Using set squares

An easy way to draw angles of 90°, 60°, 45° and 30° is with a ruler and a plastic right-angled triangle called a set square.

To draw an angle, first use a ruler to draw a line. Next, line your set square up against the ruler, with the angle you want to draw touching the ruler's edge. Then draw along the edge of the set square.

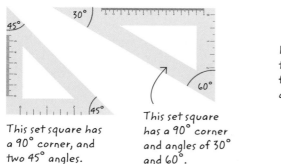

This set square has a 90° corner, and two 45° angles.

This set square has a 90° corner and angles of 30° and 60°.

Draw down this edge for a right angle.

Draw along this edge to make a 45° angle.

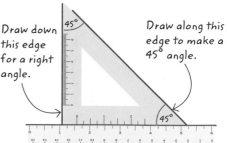

Calculating angles

You can sometimes calculate the size of an angle by using information you know. It will help if you remember the angle facts below.

Angles on straight lines

Angles on a straight line always add up to 180°. For example:

If a = 110°, then b = 70°

$$a + b = 180°$$

Perpendicular lines

Perpendicular lines always meet at 90°. For example:

If a = 90°, then b = 90°

$$a = 90°$$
$$b = 90°$$

Opposite angles

Opposite angles directly face each other and they are always the same size as each other. For example:

If a = 50°, then c = 50°
If b = 130°, then d = 130°

$$a = c$$
$$b = d$$

Angles at a point

Angles at a point always add up to 360°. For example:

If a = 100°
and b = 115°,
then c = 145°

$$a + b + c = 360°$$

Angles inside shapes

The angles inside a shape are called included angles or interior angles.

The included angles of a triangle always add up to 180°.
For example:

If a = 60°
and b = 66°,
then c = 54°

$$a + b + c = 180°$$

To test this for yourself, cut out a triangle from a piece of paper, tear off the corners and arrange them along a straight line.

The included angles of a quadrilateral add up to 360°. For example:

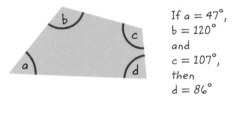

If a = 47°,
b = 120°
and
c = 107°,
then
d = 86°

$$a + b + c + d = 360°$$

To test this for yourself, cut out a quadrilateral from a piece of paper. Tear off the corners then arrange them around a point.

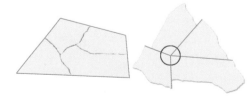

Find out more about: triangles (page 75); quadrilaterals (pages 76-77)

Measuring

You often need to measure things in everyday life, for example to find out how big or heavy they are. If everyone uses the same units to describe measurements, then people will understand the information in the same way.

Metric units

Units of length	Written as	Equal to
Millimeter	mm	
Centimeter	cm	10 millimeters
Meter	m	100 centimeters
Kilometer	km	1,000 meters

Units of capacity	Written as	Equal to
Milliliter	ml	
Centiliter	cl	100 milliliters
Liter	l	1,000 milliliters

Units of mass	Written as	Equal to
Milligram	mg	
Gram	g	1,000 milligrams
Kilogram	kg	1,000 grams

US customary units

Units of length	Written as	Equal to
Inch	" or in	
Foot	' or ft	12 inches
Yard	yd	3 feet
Mile	mi	1,760 yards

Units of capacity	Written as	Equal to
Fluid ounce	fl oz	
Pint	pt	16 fluid ounces
Quarts	qt	2 pints
Gallon	gal	8 pints

Units of mass	Written as	Equal to
Ounce	oz	
Pound	lb	16 ounces
Ton	t	2,000 pounds

Measurement systems

There are two main systems for measuring that you need to know about: the metric system and the US customary system. Each system uses different units to describe measurements.

Metric system

The metric system is decimal, which means it's based on tens, hundreds and thousands. This helps to make calculations simpler to do. Meters, grams and liters are examples of metric units. The purple box shows you the most common metric units.

US customary system

The US customary system for measuring grew out of the imperial system, which used to be the main standard of measuring in the UK. The UK now officially uses the metric system and the US typically uses the US customary system.

Inches, pounds and pints are examples of US customary units. You can see the most common US customary units in the blue box on the left.

Find out more about: capacity (page 103); **decimal system** (page 8); **length** (pages 100-101); **weight** (page 102)

Equivalent measures

You'll probably use one measuring system more than the other, but it's very useful to know what the units are roughly equal to. For example, if you know that 1 foot is roughly 30 centimeters, then if a person is 6 feet tall, their height in centimeters is about 180 cm. Here are some US customary units and their equivalent metric units.

US customary and metric units

US	Metric
Length	
1 inch	≈ 2.5 centimeters
1 foot	≈ 30 centimeters
39 inches	≈ 1 meter
$\frac{5}{8}$ mile	≈ 1 kilometer
5 miles	≈ 8 kilometers
Weight	
1 ounce	≈ 25 grams
2.2 pounds	≈ 1 kilogram
Capacity	
$1\frac{3}{4}$ pints	≈ 1 liter
1 gallon	≈ 4.5 liters

(≈ means "is roughly equal to.")

Naming metric units

The names of some metric units give you a clue about their size.

Milli... means a thousandth
For example, a millimeter is $\frac{1}{1,000}$ of a meter.

Centi... means a hundredth
For example, a centiliter is $\frac{1}{100}$ of a liter.

Kilo... means a thousand
For example, a kilogram is 1,000 grams.

Converting measurements

You often need to change or convert one unit of measurement into another, especially if you want to compare units. If you're using metric units, converting usually means dividing or multiplying by 10, 100 or 1,000.

If you want to change small units into larger ones, divide. For example:

To change 45 mm into centimeters, divide by 10 (as 1 cm = 10 mm).

$$45 \div 10 = 4.5$$

so 45 mm = 4.5 cm

To change large units into smaller ones, multiply. For example:

To change 1.2 liters into milliliters, multiply by 1,000 (as 1 l = 1,000 ml).

$$1.2 \times 1,000 = 1,200$$

so 1.2 l = 1,200 ml

If you're not sure whether to divide or multiply, try both ways and see which answer looks most sensible. For example:

A caterpillar is 20 millimeters long. How many centimeters is this?

Try $20 \times 10 = 200$

200 cm is the same as 2 m. This is taller than most adults, which is too big for a caterpillar.

Try $20 \div 10 = 2$

2 cm is about the width of two fingers. It sounds more reasonable and is the correct answer.

Find out more about: capacity (page 103); **dividing by 10, 100 and 1,000** (page 53); **length** (pages 100-101); **multiplying by 10, 100 and 1,000** (page 52); **weight** (102)

Choosing units

Math questions often tell you the units to use. But if you have to choose, use small units to measure small things and large units for larger things. For example, it's easier to imagine a ladybug that's 7 mm long than one that's 0.000007 km long. Or to imagine a playground that's 10 yards wide than one 360 inches wide.

Reading scales

Many measuring instruments, such as rulers, kitchen scales and measuring cups have lines called a scale marked on them. Numbers on the lines tell you what the measurements are, and there are often smaller marks in between, to help you measure more accurately. You will sometimes need to use decimals to write down accurate measurements.

This ruler shows centimeters and millimeters. The red line measures 4.8 cm, to the nearest millimeter.

These kitchen scales show pounds. There are 4 divisions between each 1 lb. Each division shows 0.25 lb (or 4 ounces) so you can see that the oranges weigh 20 ounces.

This pitcher holds 500 ml of liquid. The scale has 5 divisions. Each division shows 100 ml (because 500 ÷ 5 = 100 ml) so there is 300 ml of juice in the pitcher.

Always measure from the line marked 0 on a ruler, tape measure or measuring cup. Make sure the marker or display on kitchen scales is on 0 before you start.

Length

Length is the distance between two points. There are lots of units for measuring length. The ones you'll use most often are US customary units – inches (in), feet (ft), yards (yds) and miles (mi).

Remember that

1 feet	= 12 inches
1 yards	= 3 feet
1 miles	= 1,760 yards

To change	Into	Do this
inches	feet	Divide by 12
feet	inches	Multiply by 12
feet	yards	Divide by 3
feet	miles	Divide by 5,280
yards	miles	Divide by 1,760
yards	feet	Multiply by 3
miles	feet	Multiply by 5,280

Length words

There are several words for length, which mean slightly different things.

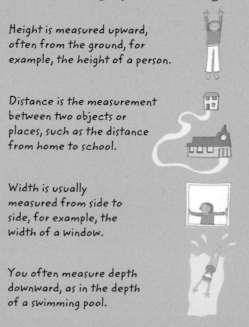

Height is measured upward, often from the ground, for example, the height of a person.

Distance is the measurement between two objects or places, such as the distance from home to school.

Width is usually measured from side to side, for example, the width of a window.

You often measure depth downward, as in the depth of a swimming pool.

The stalk of this plant is 2 inches high (its height).

The length of leaf A is $\frac{1}{2}$ inch.

Petal B is $\frac{3}{8}$ inch long.

The top of the pot is $1\frac{1}{8}$ inch wide.

Measuring lengths

Here are some instruments you can use to measure different lengths.

Measure small lengths with a ruler.

You may need a tape measure to measure longer lengths.

Use a trundle wheel for even longer lengths, such as the distance across a playground.

Longer distances still can be measured using the odometer in a car, or a bike's distance meter.

Estimating lengths

You can estimate the length of an object or distance by comparing it with the length of something you know. Always do this before you measure something, so you know roughly how big your final measurement should be. It's also handy to estimate a length if you want a rough idea of how long something is but don't have any measuring tools with you.

A finger width is about 1 cm ($\frac{3}{8}$ inch).

A 12 inch ruler is 1 foot long.

An adult is about 1.8 m tall (a little under 6 feet).

A bus is about 13 m long. That's a little over 14 yards.

You can measure parts of your body, and use these measurements to estimate lengths. It's useful to find out:

Your handspan

The length of your arm from the tip of your middle finger to your armpit.

The length of one comfortable step.

Mass and weight

Mass is the measure of how much "stuff" there is in an object. The US customary units for measuring mass are ounces (oz), pounds (lbs), and tons.

Weight measures the pull of gravity* on the stuff in an object. Scientists use special units to measure weight, but in everyday life, people use the word "weight" to mean how heavy something is and they measure it using the units of mass.

Remember that

1 pound = 16 ounces

1 ton = 2,000 pounds

To change	Into	Do this
ounces	pounds	÷16
pounds	ounces	x16
pounds	tons	÷2,000
tons	pounds	x2,000

Estimating weights

You can estimate the weight of an object by comparing it with the weight of something you already know.

A large apple weighs about 0.25 lbs, which is 4 oz.

A bag of sugar weighs 4 lbs, which is about 64 ounces.

Measuring weights

You can weigh things using a spring balance or scales.

A spring balance has a hook on the bottom, where you hang the thing you're weighing.

You can use kitchen scales like these for weighing. The measurements are written in a circle.

Or you can use balancing scales like the ones below. For example, to weigh some bananas, put the bananas in one pan, and place metal weights on the empty pan until the two pans balance.

When the pans balance, the bananas weigh the same as the weights. You can then add up the measurements written on the weights to find out how heavy the bananas are.

You'll need to weigh larger objects with larger scales, so for example, if you wanted to find out your own weight, you'd use a set of bathroom scales.

Electronic scales show weights digitally, like this.

*Gravity is a force that pulls objects toward each other, for example, Earth's gravity keeps things from floating off it into space. Your mass is the same on Earth and on the Moon, but you would weigh less on the Moon, because it has lower gravity.

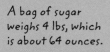

Capacity

The amount of space inside something is its capacity. For example, this might be the amount of milk in a carton or the amount of air in a balloon. The US customary units for measuring capacity are fluid ounces (fl oz), pints (pt), quarts (qt) and gallons (gal).

Remember that

1 pint	=	16 fluid ounces
1 quart	=	2 pints (or 32 fluid ounces)
1 gallon	=	4 quarts
1 gallon	=	8 pints

To change	Into	Do this
fluid ounces	pints	Divide by 16
pints	fluid ounces	Multiply by 16
fluid ounces	quarts	Divide by 32
quarts	fluid ounces	Multiply by 32
pints	gallons	Divide by 8
gallons	pints	Multiply by 8

Measuring capacity

You can use a pitcher or a measuring cup to measure capacity.

The scale on this measuring pitcher shows four divisions in every gallon. This means there are 3 quarts, 6 pints or 96 fluid ounces of water in this pitcher.

There are 1.25 pints of water in this measuring cup. That's the same as 20 fluid ounces.

Estimating capacity

You can estimate the capacity of an object by comparing it with the capacity of something you already know. It's particularly useful if you want to know roughly how much something holds but don't have a measuring cup at hand.

A tablespoon can hold about $\frac{1}{2}$ a fluid ounce of liquid.

There is about 355 ml of soft drink in a can, which is the same as 12 fluid ounces.

A 1 pint milk carton holds 16 fluid ounces.

This carton holds 2 quarts of orange juice. That's the same as 64 fluid ounces.

This fuel can holds 1 gallon, or 3.8 liters, of fuel.

Find out more about: US customary units (page 98); metric units (page 98)

Time

Time is a measurement of how long something takes. For example, it might take ten minutes to eat a meal, half an hour to walk to school or many years for a baby to reach old age.

Units of time

The units you use to measure time are based on the movement of the Earth. This is because in the days before clocks and watches, people used the position of the Sun and Moon to tell what time of day, month and year it was.

A day is the time it takes the Earth to spin around once. You can divide a day into 24 hours (hrs). Each hour contains 60 minutes (mins), and you can divide each minute into 60 seconds (s). A year is the time it takes the Earth to travel once around the Sun, and there are 12 months in a year.

You can use a calendar to find out what day of the week a particular date is.

Calendars

A calendar shows days and dates for each month of the year. Most months have 31 days, but some have 30, and February has even fewer. This rhyme will help you remember which month has what:

> 30 days have September,
> April, June and November.
> All the rest have 31,
> except for February alone,
> which has but 28 days clear
> and 29 in each leap year.

You can also use your knuckles to help you remember the lengths of months. Starting with your smallest knuckle as January, call the dip next to it February, then the next knuckle March, and so on. "Knuckle months" have 31 days, and the rest have 30, except February which has 28 days (29 in a leap year).

Units of time

1 minute	= 60 seconds
1 hour	= 60 minutes
1 day	= 24 hours
1 week	= 7 days
1 year	= 12 months
	or 52 weeks
	or 365 days
1 leap year	= 366 days
1 decade	= 10 years
1 century	= 100 years
1 millennium	= 1,000 years

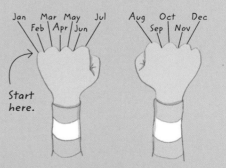

Jan Mar May Jul   Aug Oct Dec
  Feb Apr Jun   Sep Nov

Start here.

12-hour clock time

12-hour clock time divides the day into two groups of 12 hours. The first group starts at midnight (12 o'clock at night) and ends just before noon (12 o'clock in the day.) Write the letters am after these hours, for example 12:00 am, 8:30 am, 11:59 am, and so on. Hours from noon until just before midnight have the letters pm after them, for example 12:00 pm, 8:30 pm or 11:59 pm.

At 11:30 am, it is morning. *At 11:30 pm it's night.*

There are different ways to say 12-hour clock times. For example, for 3:05 am you could say, "three oh five" or "five past three." For 5:15 pm, you could say "five fifteen," "fifteen minutes past five" or "quarter past five."

Minutes past the hour...	...is also called
0	... o'clock
15	quarter past ...
30	half past ...
45	quarter to ... (the next hour)

24-hour clock time

In 24-hour clock time, or military time, you number the hours from 0 to 24. Always use 4 digits to write a 24-hour clock time. It's best to separate the hours and the minutes with a colon (:), for example, 07:26. But you'll often see times without a colon especially on travel timetables, for example, 0726. There are different ways to say 24-hour clock times. For example, 14:00 can be "fourteen hundred" or "fourteen hundred hours," and for 07:20 you could say "oh seven twenty" or "seven twenty."

Changing between 12-hour clock and 24-hour clock time

To change any 12-hour times to 24-hour clock times, drop the "am" or "pm." Most times need other changes, too. For times between 12:00 am and 12:59 am, swap the "12" of the hours for a "00," for example, 00:00 and 00:59. Write a 0 in front of single-digit hours, for example, 3:00 am becomes 03:00. Add 12 hours to times from 1:00 pm onward, so for example, 2:00 pm changes to 14:00.

To change times from 24-hour clock to 12-hour clock, you need to do the opposite. For example, subtract 12 hours from times from 13:00 to 23:59 and write "pm" after them. Take the zero off the front of times from 01:00 to 09:59 and write "am" after them. Use the chart below to check which times are equal to which, especially for times around noon and midnight.

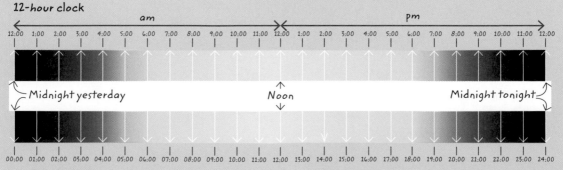

12-hour clock

| am | | | | | | | | | | | | | pm |
| 12:00 | 1:00 | 2:00 | 3:00 | 4:00 | 5:00 | 6:00 | 7:00 | 8:00 | 9:00 | 10:00 | 11:00 | 12:00 | 1:00 | 2:00 | 3:00 | 4:00 | 5:00 | 6:00 | 7:00 | 8:00 | 9:00 | 10:00 | 11:00 | 12:00 |

Midnight yesterday   Noon   Midnight tonight

00:00 01:00 02:00 03:00 04:00 05:00 06:00 07:00 08:00 09:00 10:00 11:00 12:00 13:00 14:00 15:00 16:00 17:00 18:00 19:00 20:00 21:00 22:00 23:00 24:00

24-hour clock

Find out more about: digits (page 7)

Analog clocks

On an analog clock, hands point to numbers to show the time. The small hand shows the hour and the long hand points to the minutes. When the long hand is on 12, the time is exactly "... o'clock". To work out how many minutes the long hand is showing at other times, multiply the number it is pointing to by 5.

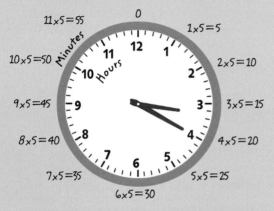

For example, the clock above is showing the time 3:20, or twenty minutes past 3 o'clock. (The long hand is pointing to 4, and 4 x 5 = 20. The short hand is pointing past the 3.)

Once you know the position of each hour on a clock, you'll be able to tell the time even if a clockface doesn't have numbers on it.

Digital clocks

Digital clocks show the time in numbers. They can show 12-hour or 24-hour time.

Here are two ways that a digital clock might show 3:20 in the afternoon.

To change	Into	Do this
seconds	minutes	÷60
minutes	hours	÷60
hours	days	÷24
minutes	seconds	x60
hours	minutes	x60
days	hours	x24

Changing units of time

To change a length of time into different units, multiply or divide it as shown in the table above. If you are dividing, and the number doesn't divide exactly, write your answer with a remainder (not as a decimal). For example:

A show lasts 140 minutes. You can find out how many hours this is by:

$140 \div 60 = 2$ remainder 20

$= 2$ hrs, 20 mins

The show lasts 2 hours, 20 minutes.

Finding the difference in time

To find the difference between two times, count on from the earlier time to the later one, starting with the smallest units. For example, if a trip begins at 6:50 pm and finishes at 9:45 pm, count up the minutes from 6:50 to the next hour (7:00 pm). Next count up the whole hours, and then add any remaining minutes to reach the final time. Add the times together to find the total length of the trip.

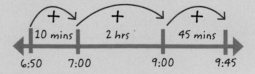

2 hrs $+ 10$ mins $+ 45$ mins

$= 2$ hrs, 55 mins

The trip lasted 2 hours, 55 minutes.

 Find out more about: **5 times table** (page 50); **12-hour clock time, 24-hour clock time** (page 105); **dividing by multiples of 10** (page 53); **hours** (page 104); **minutes** (page 104); **multiplying by multiples of 10** (page 52)

World time

The Earth is divided into different time zones. Within each time zone, people usually set their clocks to the same time. If you travel between two zones, you change your watch to the time in the new zone.

Greenwich Mean Time (GMT)

Time as measured in the London town of Greenwich is called Greenwich Mean Time or Universal Time (UT). Greenwich has an imaginary line, called the Prime Meridian Line, running through it, from the top to the bottom of the globe. Time zones to the east of the Prime Meridian Line are ahead of Greenwich Mean Time. Time zones to the west of the Prime Meridian Line are behind it.

The colors on this world map show the standard time zones, and the labels tell you how many hours ahead or behind Greenwich Mean Time each zone is. A few countries use non-standard time zones with half-hour differences. They are shown in white.

Daylight saving time

Some countries change their clocks in summer. For example in the US, everybody's clocks go forward one hour in the spring. This is called Daylight Saving Time (or DST). It is a way of helping people get more out of the days by giving them an extra hour of daylight in the evening. It also reduces the amount of energy people use because they don't use as much electricity for lights.

In the US Daylight Saving Time ends in the fall, and the clocks are turned back one hour for Local Standard Time.

International Date Line

On the other side of a globe from the Prime Meridian Line is another imaginary line called the International Date Line. In places east of the line, the date is one day earlier than it is in places west of the line.

Time zones

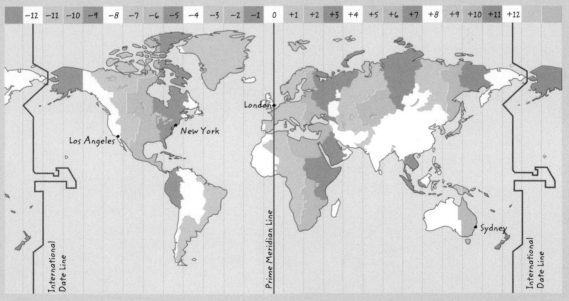

New York is in a time zone that's five hours behind GMT, so when it's 11:00 am in London, it's 6:00 am in New York. Los Angeles is eight hours behind GMT, so it would be 3:00 am there.

Sydney is in a time zone that is ten hours ahead of GMT, so when it's 1:00 pm in London, it's 11:00 pm in Sydney.

Perimeter

The distance around the edge of a shape is called its perimeter. For example, if you walk around the edges of a field, you'll walk along its perimeter. Perimeter is a length, so you'll often be asked to measure it in inches, feet or yards.

Finding a shape's perimeter

To find the perimeter of a shape, add together the lengths of all its sides.

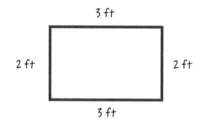

Perimeter = sum of all sides

For example, two sides of this rectangle are 3 ft long; the other two are 2 ft.

3 ft

2 ft   2 ft

3 ft

So, to find the perimeter:

3 ft + 3 ft + 2 ft + 2 ft

= 10 ft

The sides of this triangle are 2.5 ft, 3.2 ft and 4.5 ft long.

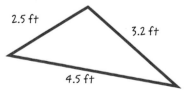

2.5 ft

3.2 ft

4.5 ft

So, to find the perimeter:

2.5 ft + 3.2 ft + 4.5 ft

= 10.2 ft

Perimeter of compound shapes

Compound shapes are made up of simpler ones. For example, the shape below is made of two rectangles. To find the perimeter of a compound shape, find the lengths of all the outside edges and add them together. For example:

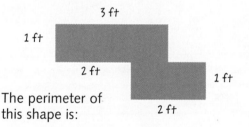

3 ft

1 ft

2 ft

1 ft

2 ft

The perimeter of this shape is:

1 ft + 3 ft + 1 ft + 1 ft + 1 ft + 2 ft
+ 1 ft + 2 ft = 12 ft

Perimeter of curved shapes

To find the perimeter of a shape with curved sides, place a piece of string along the sides until it meets, then measure the length of the string.

The length of the string tells you the perimeter of the puddle.

The perimeter of a circle is called its circumference. You can find out more about circumferences on page 79.

Find out more about: adding decimals (page 24); **length** (pages 100-101); **sides** (page 72); **sum** (page 35)

Area

Area is the amount of space a shape covers. You measure area in square units, for example, square inches (in²), square feet (ft²) or square yards (yd²) or miles (mi²).

Estimating area

To estimate the area of a shape, first draw it on a grid of squares, or draw a grid of squares over it, then count the number of squares it covers. For example, shape A covers 16 squares, so its area is 16 square units.

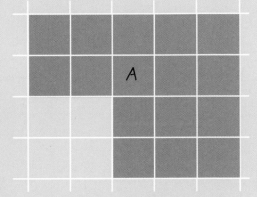

Shapes with diagonal sides

If a shape has diagonal sides, count the number of whole squares it covers, then count how many whole squares can be made from the extra pieces.

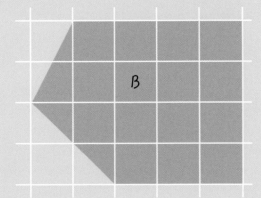

For example, shape B covers 15 whole squares and some extra pieces. These are:

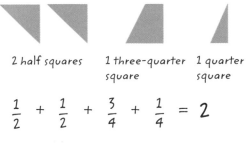

2 half squares	1 three-quarter square	1 quarter square

$$\frac{1}{2} + \frac{1}{2} + \frac{3}{4} + \frac{1}{4} = 2$$

Altogether that makes 2 more squares. So the area of shape B is 17 square units.

Shapes with curved sides

If a shape has curved sides, count the squares that are more than half covered and ignore the squares that are less than half covered. For example, shape C covers more than half of 6 squares, and less than half of 8 squares, so its area is about 6 square units.

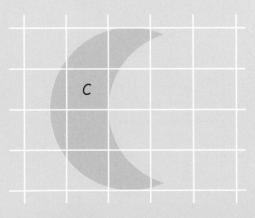

Find out more about: units of length (page 100)

Area and perimeter

Shapes with the same area can have
different perimeters. For example, each
small square below represents a field with
an area of one unit square. You could use
several different lengths of fence along the
perimeter to surround exactly 16 fields.

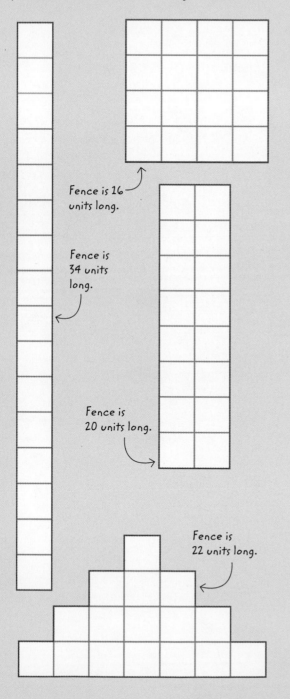

Fence is 16 units long.

Fence is 34 units long.

Fence is 20 units long.

Fence is 22 units long.

Shapes with the same perimeter can have
different areas too. For example, each
group of fields below has a fence that's
12 units long. Here you can see how many
different size groups it could surround.

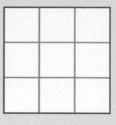

Area = 9 square units

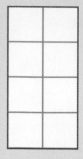

Area = 8 square units

Area = 5 square units

Conservation of area

If you cut up a shape and rearrange the
pieces, the new shape has the same area
as the original one. This idea is called
conservation of area. For example:

All these shapes have the same area.

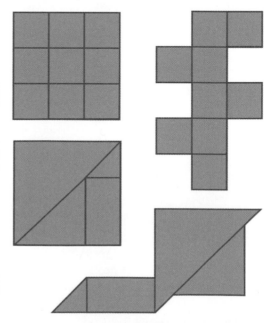

Tangrams

A tangram is an ancient Chinese shape puzzle. It has seven pieces, or tans, that fit together to form a big square. There are two large triangles, a medium one, two small ones, a square and a parallelogram.

The triangles are all right-angled isosceles triangles, so their angles are 90°, 45° and 45°.

The angles of the square are all 90°.

Two of the parallelogram's angles are 45° and the other two are 135°.

This is how all the tans fit together to form a square tangram puzzle.

The area of the large triangle is 2 x the area of the medium one.

=

The areas of the medium triangle, the square and the parallelogram are all 2 x the area of a small triangle.

=

=

=

You can use a tangram to explore the relationships between the shapes. You can make your own tangram by copying the design onto paper or cardboard and cutting it out, or downloading and printing it from the Usborne Quicklinks Website at www.usborne-quicklinks.com.

Tangram puzzles usually come with a booklet of outlines or silhouettes of all kinds of shapes, such as dogs, houses or candles. The challenge is to use all the pieces to make these shapes. This means the area of the shapes is always the same.

The tangram rules are:
- Use all seven pieces for each shape.
- The pieces must be flat.
- They must all touch.
- Pieces may not overlap.
- You can flip and/or rotate as many pieces as you like.

For example, you can rearrange the tans to make this cat shape.

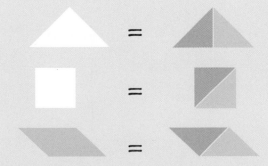

Solution

You can also use the tans to make up pictures of your own. See how many different shapes you can make. If you use all the tans, and fit them edge to edge, your pictures will all have the same area.

Find out more about: angles (pages 94-97); **area** (page 109); **parallelograms** (pages 76-77); **squares** (page 76); **triangles** (page 75)

Area of rectangles and squares

If you know the length and width of a rectangle or square, you can multiply them to find its area.

For example, you can count that the area of the rectangle below is 12 square units. Or you can multiply its width (4 units) by its length (3 units): 4 x 3 = 12.

The rule for finding the area of a rectangle or square is:

> Area = length x width

It doesn't matter which side is the length as long as the one next to it is the width. Always measure the length and width using the same units:
* If they are in inches, the area is in in^2.
* If they are in feet, the area is in ft^2.
* If they are in yards, the area is in yd^2.
* If they are in miles, the area is in mi^2.

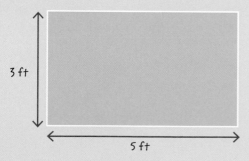

For example, this rectangle is 5 ft long and 3 ft wide, so:

Area = 5 ft x 3 ft

= 15 ft^2

Area of parallelograms

Draw a parallelogram on a piece of paper and cut a triangle off one end. If you move this triangle to the other end you make a rectangle.

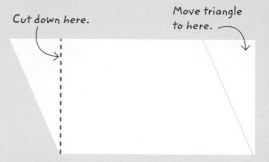

Cut down here.

Move triangle to here.

This means that the area of a parallelogram is the same as the area of a rectangle. A parallelogram's measurements are often called width and height though, so you write the rule as:

> Area = width x height

It doesn't matter which measurement you call the width as long as you call the other one the height. For example, this parallelogram is 4 in wide and 2 in high. Its area is: 4 in x 2 in = 8 in^2

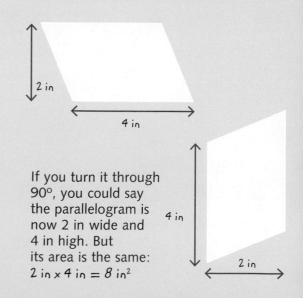

2 in

4 in

If you turn it through 90°, you could say the parallelogram is now 2 in wide and 4 in high. But its area is the same: 2 in x 4 in = 8 in^2

4 in

2 in

Area of triangles

Cut a parallelogram in half from corner to corner, and you make a pair of identical triangles. You make two triangles whichever corners you cut between.

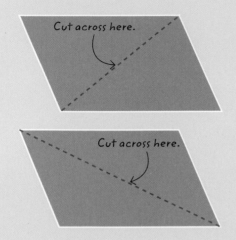

Cut across here.

Cut across here.

This means that the area of a triangle is half the area of a parallelogram. So the rule for finding the area of a triangle is half of the rule for the area of a parallelogram:

$$Area = \frac{1}{2} \times width \times height$$

For example, this triangle is 5 ft wide and 4 ft high, so:

$Area = \frac{1}{2} \times 5 \text{ ft} \times 4 \text{ ft}$
$= \frac{1}{2} \times 20 \text{ ft}$
$= 10 \text{ ft}^2$

4 ft

5 ft

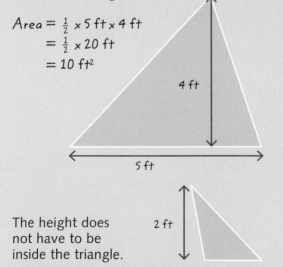

The height does not have to be inside the triangle.

2 ft

Area of quadrilaterals

You can find the area of a quadrilateral by cutting it up and finding the area of its pieces. Here are some examples:

This trapezoid is a square and two identical triangles.

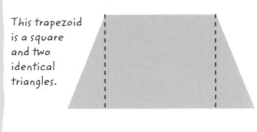

This trapezoid is a rectangle and two different triangles...

...or you could cut it up into two triangles.

You can divide a kite into two triangles, like this.

This arrowhead is made up of two triangles too.

Find out more about: arrowheads (page 77); **kites** (page 77); **parallelograms** (pages 76-77); **quadrilaterals** (pages 76-77); **trapezoids** (page 77); **triangles** (page 75)

Area of compound shapes

Compound shapes are made up of simpler ones. To find the area of a compound shape, find the area of each of the shapes in it and add them together. For example, the shape below is made of a square and a rectangle.

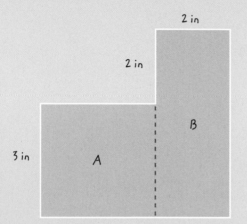

To find its area:
* find the area of A
* find the area of B
* add the areas together.

Area of square A
= length x width
= 3 in x 3 in
= 9 in²

Area of rectangle B
= length x width
= 2 in x 5 in
= 10 in²

Area of shape
= area of A + area of B
= 9 in² + 10 in²
= 19 in²

So the area of the shape is 19 in².

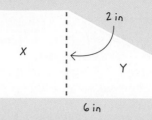

The shape above is made of a square and a triangle. To find its area:
* find the area of X
* find the area of Y
* add the areas together.

Area of square X
= length x width
= 2 in x 2 in
= 4 in²

Area of triangle Y
= ½ x base x height
= ½ x 4 in x 2 in
= ½ x 8 in²
= 4 in²

Area of shape = area of X + area of Y
= 4 in² + 4 in² = 8 in²

So the area of the shape is 8 in².

Area of circles

The rule for finding the area of a circle is:

$$Area = \pi \times radius^2 \text{ or } \pi r^2$$
π stands for the number Pi, which is about 3.142.

For example, the area of this circle is:
3.142 x 2 in x 2 in
= 12.57 in² (2 d.p.)

Surface area

The surface area of a 3-D shape is all of its outer surface. For example, the surface area of a pear is all its outer skin.

To find the surface area of a polygon, first find the area of each face. Then add all these areas together. For example:

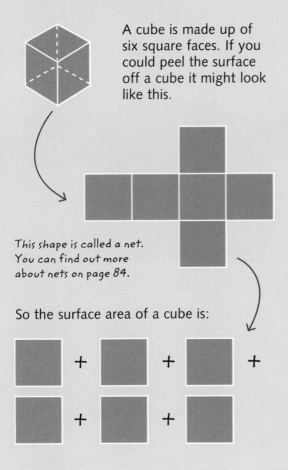

A cube is made up of six square faces. If you could peel the surface off a cube it might look like this.

This shape is called a net. You can find out more about nets on page 84.

So the surface area of a cube is:

2 in

To find the surface area of this cube, first find the area of one face:
$2 \text{ in} \times 2 \text{ in} = 4 \text{ in}^2$

The cube has 6 faces, so you need to multiply the area of one face by 6:
$6 \times 4 \text{ in}^2 = 24 \text{ in}^2$

So the surface area of the cube is 24 in².

A cuboid has six faces. Two of them are squares and four are rectangles.

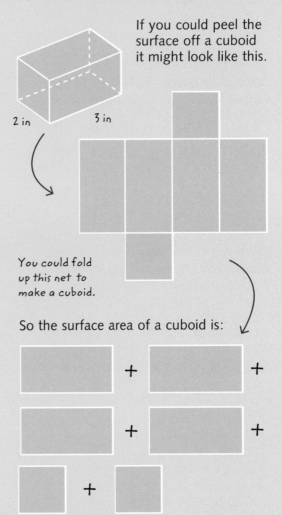

If you could peel the surface off a cuboid it might look like this.

2 in   3 in

You could fold up this net to make a cuboid.

So the surface area of a cuboid is:

To find the surface area of the cuboid, first find the area of a rectangular face:
$2 \text{ in} \times 3 \text{ in} = 6 \text{ in}^2$
Multiply it by 4: $4 \times 6 \text{ in}^2 = 24 \text{ in}^2$

Next find the area of one square face
$2 \text{ in} \times 2 \text{ in} = 4 \text{ in}^2$
Multiply it by 2: $2 \times 4 \text{ in}^2 = 8 \text{ in}^2$

Add together the areas of the rectangular faces and square faces:
$24 \text{ in}^2 + 8 \text{ in}^2 = 32 \text{ in}^2$

The cuboid's surface area is 32 in².

Find out more about: 3-D shapes (pages 81-84); **cubes** (page 82); **cuboids** (page 82)

Volume

Volume is the amount of 3-D space a 3-D shape takes up. You measure volume in cubic units, for example cubic inches (in³), cubic feet (ft³) or cubic yards (yd³).

Units of volume

Most units you use to measure volume are related to units of length. For example, the cube below measures 1 ft on each side, so its volume is 1 cubic feet (1 ft³). A cubic yard (1 yd³) measures 1 yd x 1 yd x 1 yd, and so on.

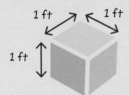

1 ft

1 ft

1 ft

1 ft x 1 ft x 1 ft
= 1 cubic foot
You can also write
this as 1 ft³.

You can find the volume of a solid by counting how many unit cubes you could fit inside it. For example, you could fit 36 unit cubes inside the cuboid below, so its volume is 36 cubic units.

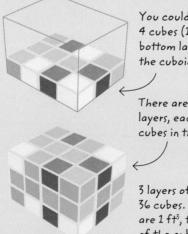

You could fit 3 by 4 cubes (12) on the bottom layer of the cuboid.

There are two more layers, each with 12 cubes in them.

3 layers of 12 cubes is 36 cubes. If the cubes are 1 ft³, the volume of the cuboid is 36 ft³.

Finding the volume of cuboids

The rule for finding the volume of a cuboid is:

> Volume of a cuboid
> = length x width x height

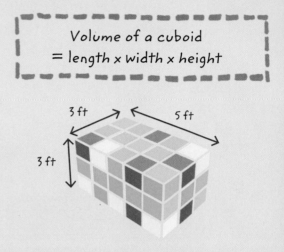

3 ft

5 ft

3 ft

For example, the volume of this cuboid is:
3 ft x 5 ft x 3 ft = 45 ft³

Finding the volume of cubes

You can use the rule for the volume of a cuboid to calculate the volume of a cube. All the sides of a cube are the same length, so you can write the rule as:

> Volume of a cube
> = side x side x side = side³

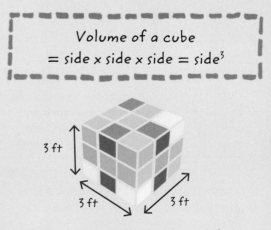

3 ft

3 ft

3 ft

For example, the volume of this cube is:
3 ft x 3 ft x 3 ft = 27 ft³

Find out more about: 3-D shapes (pages 81-84); **units of length** (page 100)

Handling data

Data is another name for information. Handling data means collecting it, finding out what it can tell you and showing it to other people in a way that's easy for them to understand.

Discrete data

Data that can only have particular values, for example, the number of children in a class, is called discrete data. The number of children is discrete data because you can only count them in whole numbers (you can't have half a child). Popcorn carton sizes can be another example of discrete data, for instance when you have to choose a small, medium or large one. You usually collect discrete data by counting.

Continuous data

Data that can have any value within a range is called continuous data. For example, the heights of children in class 4H range from 47 inches to 52 inches. This is continuous data because each child can measure any value in between.

Collecting data

You can gather most data by watching or measuring something, or by asking questions. For example, you can count how many red cars drive past your school one lunchtime, measure how far a ball is thrown in a competition, or ask your friends what their favorite book is.

Data you've collected yourself is primary data. If someone else collected it, it's secondary data. You can keep a record of your data on a sheet called a data collection sheet. Then you can put the data into charts or graphs and study it. The type of math that involves gathering and recording data is called statistics.

Surveys

A survey is a way of collecting information from some members of a group of people, and using their answers to tell you about the whole group. For example, instead of asking everyone in your school what breakfast cereal they eat on Tuesdays, you could ask 100 people. If 33 of them have cornflakes, this could mean that about 33% of children in the school eat cornflakes on Tuesdays.

Questionnaires

A questionnaire is a list of questions used in surveys. The best questionnaires are short and clear. The writers often limit the range of answers in some way. This makes it easier for them to sort and compare the results. For example:

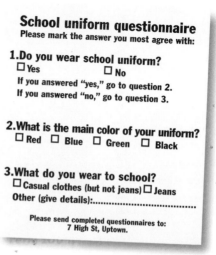

School uniform questionnaire
Please mark the answer you most agree with:

1. Do you wear school uniform?
   ☐ Yes   ☐ No
   If you answered "yes," go to question 2.
   If you answered "no," go to question 3.

2. What is the main color of your uniform?
   ☐ Red   ☐ Blue   ☐ Green   ☐ Black

3. What do you wear to school?
   ☐ Casual clothes (but not jeans) ☐ Jeans
   Other (give details):.............................

Please send completed questionnaires to:
7 High St, Uptown.

Find out more about: charts and graphs (pages 119-123)

Data lists

A data list shows each piece of information as you get it. Data like this is raw data, which means you need to sort it before you can see anything useful.

2	1	3	2	1	1
3	2	1	1	1	2
1	1	2	4	1	1

This data list shows how many people were in each car that passed a school gate one lunchtime.

Tally charts

You can collect and sort data on a tally chart by drawing a little line, called a tally, to show each item you count. Write the fifth tally in each group across, like a gate, to make it easier to add them. By adding up the tallies in each row, you can see the frequency – the number of times the same piece of information occurs.

Class 4B birthdays

Month	Tally	Frequency
January	II	2
February	I	1
March	II	2
April	IIII I	6
May	III	3
June	IIII	4
July	II	2
August	II	2
September	IIII	5
October	II	2
November		0
December	II	2

This tally chart shows the birthdays of children in class 4B. By counting the tallies you can easily see that six children have April birthdays.

Grouping data

Sometimes it can help you understand information if you put the data into groups. For example, 35 children played a computer game and made a data list of their scores:

14	25	8	47	21
36	29	36	42	17
7	32	38	26	33
15	24	13	30	16
35	41	5	19	32
31	30	36	40	10
29	35	31	28	22

You can group the scores together and use a tally chart to show how many children scored in each group. Add up the tallies to find the frequency for each group.

Scores

Score	Tally	Frequency
1–10	IIII	4
11–20	IIII I	6
21–30	IIII IIII	10
31–40	IIII IIII II	12
41–50	III	3

Now you can look at the data and easily see which is the highest scoring range. (Most children scored between 31 and 40 points.) The information shows that it's much harder to score 41 or more, as only 3 children out of 35 managed it.

Each group of data in the table is called a class interval. For example the first class interval in the table above is 1–10.

Sharing data

Once you have collected and sorted your data, you can use diagrams or charts to show, or represent, your information. This helps people to understand the data, just by looking at it.

Pictograms

A pictogram uses pictures or symbols to display information. Each symbol represents an amount, and you can use part of a symbol to show a smaller amount. For example, the pictogram on the right represents the data on the tally chart above it, and shows the number of ice cream cones a café sold in one week.

Here are some things you need to do to make pictograms clear and easy to understand:

1. Give your pictogram a title, to tell people what it is showing.

2. Write a key to explain what the symbols mean.

3. Make your symbols the same size.

4. Draw them in a line and space them out evenly, so you can see at a glance which row has the most symbols in it.

5. If you use different symbols, make sure they are the same size as each other and represent the same number of items. For example:

Ice cream cones sold in a week

Day	Tally	Frequency
Monday	IIII I	6
Tuesday	IIII	5
Wednesday	IIII	4
Thursday	II	2
Friday	IIII I	6
Saturday	IIII III	8
Sunday	IIII III	8

Key

= 2 ice cream cones

= 2 ice pops

= 2 hot dogs

Bar charts

A bar chart uses bars to show frequency. The bars are the same width, but their heights vary with the frequency they're showing. It's important that the numbers on the vertical axis go up evenly. Always give your bar chart a title, and label the axes with what you are showing and the units you're measuring in. For example:

Bar charts with vertical (upright) bars are sometimes called column graphs or block graphs. You'll also see charts with horizontal bars or lines. For example, the bar chart below shows the same data as the one on the left, but the frequency (the number of children) is on the horizontal axis instead of the vertical one.

Favorite milkshake flavors of class 4H

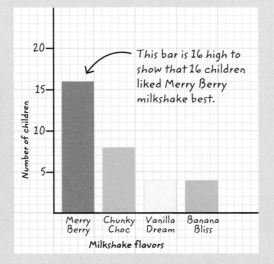

This bar is 16 high to show that 16 children liked Merry Berry milkshake best.

Favorite milkshake flavors of class 4H

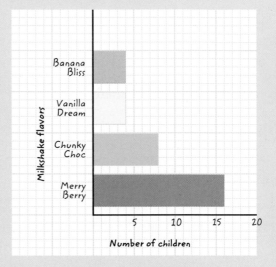

A bar line chart or bar line graph uses lines instead of bars to show frequency. For example:

You can use a bar chart to show grouped data too, as long as you make sure that the groups have the same range. For example:

Favorite milkshake flavors of class 4H

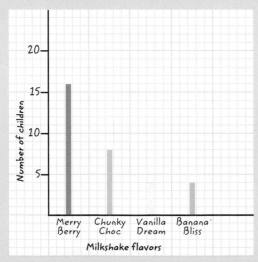

Time taken to travel to school

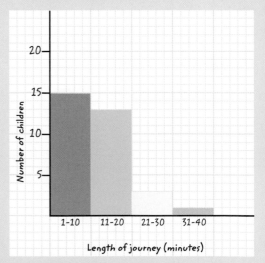

Pie charts

A pie chart gets its name from its round shape. Each "slice" of the pie represents a category, and the size of the slice represents the frequency of the data. The bigger the slice, the higher the frequency, so pie charts are a good way of showing at a glance how something is divided up. Remember to add a title and labels, or a key, to tell you what the pie chart is showing. For example:

Favorite milkshake flavors of class 4H

Sophie asked 32 children in her class their favorite milkshake flavor, and put the results in a pie chart. If you look at the fraction of the pie each slice represents, you can work out roughly how many of the children preferred each flavor. For example:

Merry Berry is half of the pie, which means that half of the children chose Merry Berry milkshake.

$$\frac{1}{2} \times 32 = 16$$

So Merry Berry was the favorite flavor of 16 children.

Chunky Chocolate is a quarter of the pie, which means that 8 children preferred it (because $\frac{1}{4} \times 32 = 8$).

Sorting diagrams

You can sometimes use sorting diagrams to show how numbers, shapes or other information relate to each other.

Carroll diagrams

To sort information using a Carroll diagram you need to decide which box each item should go in. For example, you could use the categories in the boxes below to sort these shapes:

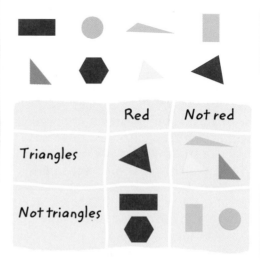

Venn diagrams

A Venn diagram uses circles to show the relationship between sets of information. For example:

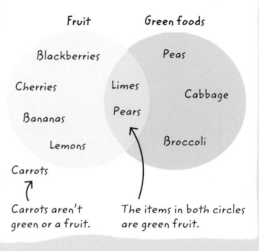

Carrots aren't green or a fruit.

The items in both circles are green fruit.

Line graphs

A line graph shows information using straight lines to join together a set of points on a grid. Add a title to tell people what the graph shows, and labels to explain what the axes represent.

For example, the line graph below shows a sporting goods store's monthly sales of bikes. The position of the points up the vertical axis shows how many bikes the store sold. Their position along the horizontal axis shows the months they sold them. So you can "read" the points to find out how many bikes were sold in a particular month.

For example, to find out how many bikes were sold in January, find the January label on the horizontal axis, and use a ruler to go straight up from it until you touch the line. Then use your ruler to follow in a straight line from this point across to the vertical axis, and read the number on the scale. This tells you that in January, the store sold 100 bikes. You can use the same method to see how many bikes they sold in other months.

You can use crosses or x's to show points on a line graph. On many line graphs, the lines between points don't show any real values, but the slope of the lines shows the trend. This means it gives you an idea of how the values of the points are changing. For example:

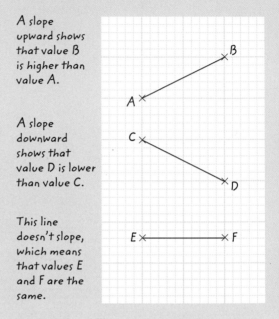

A slope upward shows that value B is higher than value A.

A slope downward shows that value D is lower than value C.

This line doesn't slope, which means that values E and F are the same.

The steeper the slope, the greater the rate of change, so a steep slope shows a bigger change than a shallow one.

Monthly sale of bikes

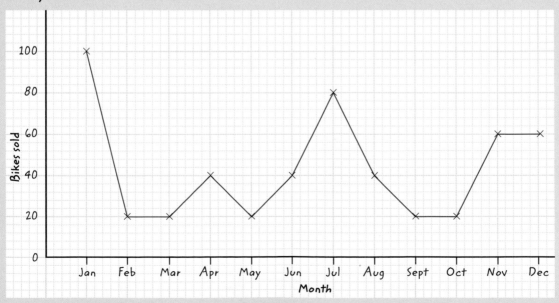

Distance-time graphs

Distance-time graphs (or travel graphs) show how far something has moved in a certain time.

For example, the distance-time graph below shows Tom's journey to school one morning. The vertical axis shows how far he traveled, while the horizontal axis shows the time of his journey.

Tom's journey to school

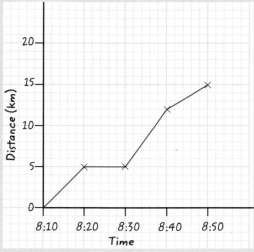

The steeper the line, the faster an object is traveling. For example:

Object A is moving faster than object B, which in turn is faster than object C.

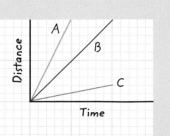

So, you can see from Tom's graph that his journey was quickest between 8:30 and 8:40, but between 8:20 and 8:30, he didn't move at all. (Maybe the traffic was bad or the bus stopped to pick up lots of people.)

Conversion graphs

A conversion graph helps you change one unit into another. It works because the units change value at the same rate. For example, if one US dollar is equal to £0.75, then two dollars are equal to £1.50 (which is 2 x £0.75), and so on. For example, on the conversion graph below, one American dollar is equal to two European euros.

Exchange rate from American dollars to euros

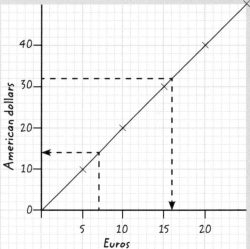

You read conversion graphs in the same way as line graphs. For example, to change 32 dollars to euros, read up the scale on the vertical axis and work out which line shows 32 dollars. Then read straight across to the line and straight down to the horizontal axis to see how many euros they're worth (16).

To convert euros to dollars, start on the horizontal axis, read up to the line and back to the vertical axis. So on this graph, 7 euros are worth 14 dollars.

Remember, on conversion graphs, every point along the line has a value.

Find out more about: axes (page 91); **horizontal** (page 91); **lines** (page 71); **points** (page 71); **vertical** (page 91)

Averages

An average is a piece of information that you use to represent a whole set of data. For example, if a group of children are aged 9, 9, 10, 9, 8, 9, 9, 8, 9 and 10, it quicker and more useful for their teacher to say their average age is 9. There are three different kinds of average: mode, mean and median.

Mode

The mode is the value or item that occurs most often in a set of data. It's useful to find the mode if you want to know what the most common or popular result is.

For example, this tally chart shows the favorite computer sports game of 30 children. Finding the mode will tell you which game is the most popular.

Sport	Tally
Go-cart racing	IIII IIII
Hula-hooping	III
Balancing games	II
Tennis	IIII
Baseball	IIII
Skiing	IIII II

If you add up the tallies, you'll see that the most common result is go-cart racing, which was the favorite game of 10 children. This means that the mode of the data is go-cart racing.

You can remember which type of average the mode is because "mode" sounds a little like "most."

Mean

The mean is a typical value of a set of data. To find the mean of a list of values, add them all up then divide by the number of values there are. You can write this as:

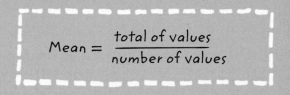

$$\text{Mean} = \frac{\text{total of values}}{\text{number of values}}$$

For example, here are the temperatures of a vacation resort during a week in June.

	M	T	W	T	F	S	S
°F	78	79	80	79	81	82	81

To find the mean temperature:

$78 + 79 + 80 + 79 + 81 + 82 + 81$

$= 560$

$\frac{560}{7} = 80$

The mean temperature was 80°F.

If someone tells you an average, but they don't say which kind, they usually mean the mean.

Median

The middle value in a set of data is called the median. It's a useful average if the data has a few values that are much higher or lower than the rest.

For example, to find the median of these quiz scores:

5 49 37 51 45 62 73 98 35

First list them in order, starting with the smallest. Then find the middle value.

5 35 37 45 (49) 51 62 73 98

The middle value is 49 so this is the median score.

If there's an even number of values, the median is halfway between the two middle values. To find it, find the middle two values, add them together and divide the result by 2.

For example, if the scores are:

5 35 37 45 (49)(51) 54 62 73 98

The middle values are 49 and 51. To find the median:

$(49 + 51) \div 2$
$= 100 \div 2$
$= 50$

The median score is 50.

> You can remember which type of average the median is because "median" sounds a little like "middle."

Range

The range of a set of data is the difference between the largest and smallest values. To find the range, put the values in order, starting with the smallest, then subtract the smallest number from the largest. You can write this as:

> $$\text{Range} = \text{highest value} - \text{lowest value}$$

For example, to find the range of these exam scores:

31 21 38 30 27 48 33 36 24

First list the scores in order, starting with the smallest. Then subtract the lowest value from the highest:

21 24 27 30 31 33 36 38 48

$\text{Range} = 48 - 21 = 27$

To find the range of grouped data, subtract the lowest possible value from the highest possible value.

For example, this chart shows the ages of a group of 30 children.

Age (years)	Tally	Frequency
5–8	ЖЖ III	8
9–12	ЖЖ ЖЖ III	13
13–16	ЖЖ IIII	9

The youngest a child in this group can be is 5 and the oldest is 16, so the range is 11 years (16 – 5).

Find out more about: subtracting (pages 35-45)

Chance and probability

Probability is the measurement of how likely something is to happen. Most people use probability words every day. For example, you might say you'll definitely meet your friend after school or it's impossible to finish all your homework before dinner. Another word for probability is chance.

Events

When you're talking about probability, something that happens is known as an event. For example, rolling a dice or tossing a coin is an event.

Outcomes

The result of an event is its outcome. The score you get if you throw a dice, or which way up a coin lands if you toss it are both examples of outcomes.

Equally likely outcomes

If something is just as likely to happen as it is not to happen, you say its probability is an even chance. You might also call it a fifty-fifty chance. For example, if you toss a coin, you're equally likely to get heads as tails.

Probability scale

You can show the probability of outcomes on a probability scale like the one at the bottom of this page. The scale ranges from impossible to certain and there are lots of words you can use to describe how likely something is to happen.

The probability scale is measured from 0 to 1. An impossible outcome has a probability of 0, and a certain outcome has a probability of 1. Everything else is in between.

You can show probability as a fraction, decimal, percentage or ratio, too. For example, an equally likely outcome has a probability of $\frac{1}{2}$, 0.5 or 50%. You could also say that it has a 1 in 2 chance or a 50:50 chance.

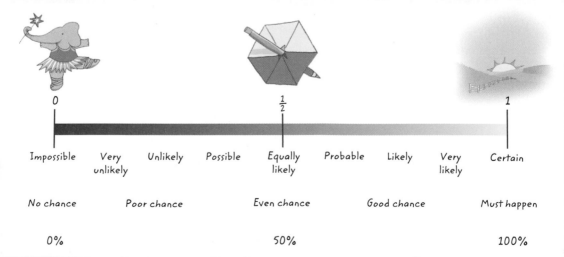

0				$\frac{1}{2}$					1
Impossible	Very unlikely	Unlikely	Possible	Equally likely	Probable	Likely	Very likely		Certain
No chance		Poor chance		Even chance		Good chance			Must happen
0%				50%					100%

Random

Events that are random all have an equal chance of happening. For example, lottery results are random because each numbered ball has an equal chance of being picked in each draw.

Coin probability

If you toss a coin there are two possible outcomes: it could land on heads or tails. There is an even chance (1 in 2) of it landing on heads and an even chance of tails.

Tossing two coins gives you four possible outcomes:

Outcome 1

Outcome 2

Outcome 3

Outcome 4

The chance of both coins showing tails is 1 in 4. There are two different ways you could throw a head and a tail, so the probability of throwing a head and a tail is 2 in 4. You can simplify this by dividing each number by 2, so the probability of throwing a head and a tail is 1 in 2.

Dice probability

Dice have six sides, each with a different number of spots on it: 1, 2, 3, 4, 5 and 6. This means that the chance of throwing each number is 1 in 6.

There are three odd numbers (1, 3, 5), so the chance of throwing an odd number is 3 in 6. This can be simplified to 1 in 2, which is an even chance.

There are five numbers (1, 2, 3, 4, 5) that are not 6, so the chance of throwing a number that is not a 6 is 5 in 6.

The probability of rolling a dice and getting a six is $\frac{1}{6}$.

The probability of rolling a number that is not a six is $\frac{5}{6}$.

This is equal to $1 - \frac{1}{6}$.

Fair and unfair

If you throw a dice over and over, it should show each face a similar number of times. If this happens, the dice is fair. But if you throw, say, a lot more sixes than ones, you might say the dice is unfair or biased.

Find out more about: simplifying ratios (page 29)

Math symbols

Here are some useful math symbols that you need to recognize. In the list, the letters n and m stand for any numbers or values that you might see with the symbols.

+ Addition sign
(see page 35) For example:

$$2 + 5 = 7$$

= Equals sign
(see page 31) For example:

$$2 + 3 = 6 - 1$$

− Subtraction sign
(see page 35) For example:

$$13 - 4 = 9$$

≠ Is not equal to sign
For example:

$$2 + 2 \neq 5$$

X Multiplication sign
(see page 46) For example:

$$6 \times 5 = 30$$

< Less than sign
(see page 31) For example:

$$1 < 3$$

÷ Division sign
(see page 46) For example:

$$12 \div 3 = 4$$

> More than sign
(see page 31) For example:

$$3 > 1$$

+n Positive number
(see page 7) For example:

$$+2 \times +3 = +6$$
$$or\ just: 2 \times 3 = 6$$

≤ Less than or equal to
For example:

$$+n \leq 3$$
$$so\ n = 1, 2\ or\ 3$$

−n Negative number
(see page 7) For example:

$$0 - 1 = -1$$

≥ More than or equal to
For example:

$$n \geq 3$$
$$so\ n = 3, 4, 5...$$

≈ **Is approximately equal to sign**
(see page 34) For example:

$$10 \div 3 \approx 3$$

n^2 **Squared number**
(see page 10) For example:

$$2^2 = 2 \times 2 = 4$$

n^3 **Cubed number**
(see page 10) For example:

$$2^3 = 2 \times 2 \times 2 = 8$$

$\sqrt{n}$ **Square root sign**
(see page 12) For example:

$$\sqrt{4} = 2$$

$\sqrt[3]{n}$ **Cube root sign**
(see page 12) For example:

$$\sqrt[3]{8} = 2$$

% **Percentage sign**
(see page 25) For example:

$$25\% \times 12 = 3$$

n:m **Ratio**
(see page 29) For example:

In a parking lot, the ratio of wheels to cars is 4:1.

• **Decimal point**
(see page 21) For example:

$$15 \div 2 = 7.5$$

$\bar{n}$ **Recurring number**
(see page 21) For example:

$$10 \div 3 = 3.\bar{3}$$

$n°$ **Degrees sign**
(see page 94) For example:

A right angle is 45°.

⌐ **Right angle sign**
(see page 94) For example:

(n) **Parentheses**
(see page 62) For example:

$$2 \times (5 - 1)$$
$$= 2 \times 4 = 8$$

π **Pi (approximately 3.142)**
(see page 79) For example:

Circumference of a circle
$= \pi \times$ diameter

∞ **Infinity sign**
(see page 7) For example:

$$1 \div 0 = \infty$$

Index

Acknowledgements

Cover designer: Kate Rimmer
Web researcher: Sarah Khan
Additional illustrations by Keith Furnival